PROJECT SUCCESS 5

Steve Gwynne
Ingrid Greenberg
Jennifer Bixby

Series Consultants
Susan Gaer
Sarah Lynn

The publisher would like to thank Irene Frankel for her creative conception and vision for this groundbreaking course.

PROJECT SUCCESS 5

Copyright © 2014 by Pearson Education, Inc.

Pearson Education, 10 Bank Street, White Plains, NY 10606

Staff Credits: The people who made up the *Project Success* team, representing editorial, production, design, and manufacturing, are Peter Benson, Andrea Bryant, Maretta Callahan, Iris Candelaria, Aerin Csigay, Mindy DePalma, Dave Dickey, Christine Edmonds, Nancy Flaggman, Ann France, Aliza Greenblatt, Gosia Jaros-White, Caroline Kasterine, Amy Kefauver, Niki Lee, Jaime Lieber, Jessica Miller-Smith, Tracey Munz Cataldo, Laurie Neaman, Jenn Raspiller, Julie Schmidt, Kim Snyder, Katherine Sullivan, Loretta Steeves, Jane Townsend, Ken Volcjak, and Martin Yu.

Interior Design: Word & Image

Cover Design: Ann France and Tracey Munz Cataldo

Text Composition: TSI Graphics

Text font: Franklin Gothic

For photo and illustration credits, please turn to the back of the book.

Library of Congress Cataloging-in-Publication Data
Lynn, Sarah.
  Project success : skills for the 21st century / Sarah Lynn ; Series Consultants: Susan Gaer, Sarah Lynn.
      pages cm
  Summary: Project Success is a blended-learning digital and print course with a strong focus on workplace skills, career readiness, and 21st century challenges. This unique video-based series engages learners with high-interest video vignettes that represent a "day in the life" of characters in diverse workplace settings that may simulate their own. Integrated skills lessons encourage critical thinking and problem solving woven into the students' English language learning journey.
  ISBN 978-0-13-294236-2 — ISBN 978-0-13-248297-4 — ISBN 978-0-13-294238-6 — ISBN 978-0-13-294240-9 — ISBN 978-0-13-294242-3 — ISBN 978-0-13-298513-0
  1. English language—Textbooks for foreign speakers. 2. English language—Spoken English. 3. English language—Sound recordings for foreign speakers. 4. English language—Study and teaching—Foreign speakers—Audio-visual aids. 5. Business communication—United States—Vocational guidance. I. Gaer, Susan. II. Title.
  PE1128.L98 2014
  428.2'4—dc23
                                                                2013035851

ISBN-10: 0-13-298513-6
ISBN-13: 978-0-13-298513-0

Printed in the United States of America
1 2 3 4 5 6 7 8 9 10—V082—19 18 17 16 15 14

Contents

Acknowledgments

The authors and publisher would like to offer sincere thanks to our Series Consultants for lending their expertise and insights and for helping shape the course.

Susan Gaer Santa Ana College School of Continuing Education, Santa Ana, CA

Sarah Lynn Harvard Bridge to Learning and Literacy Program, Cambridge, MA

In addition, we would like to express gratitude to the following people. Their kind participation was invaluable to the creation of this program.

Consultants

Robert Breitbard, Director of Adult & Community Education, Collier County Public Schools, Naples, Florida; **Ingrid Greenberg**, Associate Professor, ESL, and Past-President, Academic Senate, Continuing Education, San Diego Community College District, San Diego, California; **Vittoria G. Maghsoudi-Abbate**, Assistant Director, Mt. Diablo Adult Education, Mt. Diablo USD, Concord, California; **Irina Patten**, Lone Star College-Fairbanks Center, Houston, Texas; **Maria Soto Caratini**, Eastfield College DCCCD, Mesquite, Texas; **Claire Valier**, Palm Beach County, Florida; **Jacqueline S. Walpole**, Director, Adult Education, Prince George's Community College, Largo, Maryland.

Reviewers

Eleanor Brockman-Forfang, Instructor, Special Projects (ESL), Tarrant County College, South Campus, Fort Worth, TX; **Natalya Dollar**, ESL Program Resource Coordinator, North Orange County Community College District, Anaheim, CA; **Bette Empol**, ESL, ABE, GED Prep and Bridge Coordinator, Conejo Valley Adult School, Thousand Oaks, CA; **Mark Fisher**, Lone Star College-Fairbanks Center, Houston, TX; **Ann Fontanella**, ESL Instructor, City College of San Francisco, San Francisco, CA; **Ingrid Greenberg**, Associate Professor, ESL, and Past-President, Academic Senate, Continuing Education, San Diego Community College District, San Diego, CA; **Janet Harclerode**, Santa Monica College, Santa Monica, CA; **Laura Jensen**, ESL Instructor, North Seattle Community College, Seattle, WA; **Tommie Martinez**, Fresno Adult School, Fresno, CA; **Suzanne L. Monti**, ESOL Instructional Specialist, Community College of Baltimore County, Continuing Education, Baltimore, MD; **Kelly Nusz**, Carlos Rosario Charter School, Washington, D.C; **Irina Patten**, Lone Star College-Fairbanks Center, Houston, TX; **Ariel Peckokas**, Collier County Public Schools Adult Education, Naples, FL; **Sydney Rice**, Imperial Valley College, Imperial, CA; **Richard Salvador**, McKinley Community Schools of Arts, Honolulu, Hawaii; **Maria Soto Caratini**, Eastfield College DCCCD, Mesquite, TX; **Patty Swartzbaugh**, Nashville Adult Literacy Council, Nashville, TN; **Candace Thompson-Lynch**, ESL Instructor, School of Continuing Education, North Orange County Community College District, Anaheim, CA; **Esther M. Tillet**, Miami Dade College-Wolfson Campus, Miami, FL; **Adriana Treadway**, Assistant Director, Spring International Language Center, University of Arkansas, Fayetteville, AR; **Monica C. Vazquez**, ESOL Adjunct Instructor, Brookhaven College, DCCCD, Farmers Branch, TX.

Thanks also to the teachers who contributed their valuable ideas for the Persistence Activities: **Dave Coleman**, Los Angeles Unified School District, Los Angeles, CA; **Renee Collins**, Elk Grove Adult and Community Education, Elk Grove, CA; **Elaine Klapman**, Venice Community Adult School, Venice, CA (retired); **Yvonne Wong Nishio**, Evans Community Adult School, Los Angeles, CA; **Daniel S. Pittaway**, North Orange County Community College District, Anaheim, CA; **Laurel Pollard**, Educational Consultant, Tucson, AZ; **Eden Quimzon**, Santiago Canyon College, Division of Continuing Education, Orange, CA.

Special thanks also to **Sharon Goldstein** for her skilled writing of the pronunciation strand.

SERIES CONSULTANTS

Susan Gaer has worked as an ESL teacher since 1980 and currently teaches at the Santa Ana College School of Continuing Education. She is an avid user of technology and trains teachers online for TESOL and the Outreach Technical Assistance Center (OTAN). Susan is a frequent presenter at local, state, national, and international conferences on using the latest technology with adult learners from the literacy level through transition to college. She has co-authored books and teacher's manuals, served on the executive boards for CATESOL (California Teachers of English to Speakers of Other Languages) and TESOL, and contributed to standing committees for professional development and technology. Susan holds a master's degree in English with emphasis in TESOL from San Francisco State University and a master's degree in Educational Technology from Pepperdine University.

Sarah Lynn has over twenty-five years of teaching experience in ESOL. She has dedicated much of her teaching life to working with low-level learners with interrupted education. Currently she teaches at the Harvard Bridge Program, Harvard University. As a teacher trainer, Sarah has led professional development workshops throughout the United States on topics such as teaching in the multilevel classroom, learner persistence, twenty-first-century skills, self-directed learning, collaborative learning, and scaffolding learning for the literacy learner. As a consultant, she has written ESOL curricula for programs in civics, literacy, phonics, and English language arts. As a materials writer, she has contributed to numerous Pearson ELT publications, including *Business Across Cultures, Future, Future U.S. Citizens*, and *Project Success*. Sarah holds a master's degree in TESOL from Teacher's College, Columbia University.

AUTHORS

Steve Gwynne has been teaching ESL for San Diego Continuing Education since 1991. He began his career in small business before entering teaching. An innovator in integrating technology and language learning, he has presented at conferences and conducted workshops, and he also has created websites to support EL Civics and VESL instruction. Additionally, he helped develop innovative workplace curricula for private industry and taught in a blended synchronous instructional mode. While teaching, he earned a master's Degree in TESOL from Alliant International University. Currently, he is an Assistant Program Chair at Mid-City Center where he also teaches Advanced ESL, VESL, and produces an online ESL newsletter.

Ingrid Greenberg is an award-winning educator, consultant, and author of numerous ESL and Workplace ESL articles, curricula, and textbooks. She is a dynamic facilitator who has trained thousands of professionals to design and implement ESL technology, curriculum, and assessment tools. She frequently speaks on educational policy and technology while serving as the Academic Senate President of the largest continuing education program affiliated with a California community college. She has provided educational management solutions for Fortune 500 companies and local companies in several industries, including hotel & hospitality, food services, shipyards, and construction. She earned a B.A. from University of California, San Diego and a M.A. in Linguistics from San Diego State University (SDSU). She is currently pursuing a second M.A. in Educational Technology at SDSU. Her Continuing Education colleagues recognized her with the Faculty Recognition Award for Empowering and Dedicated Teaching.

Jennifer Bixby holds an M.A. in TESOL from Boston University. She has been an ELT teacher in Colombia, Japan, and in the U.S. in a wide variety of programs, including private language academies, community colleges, and intensive programs. An experienced ELT writer and editor, she has co-authored several dual-skills books and is a contributing writer on a number of ELT textbooks. Her interests are in teaching reading and writing, and she often presents at TESOL.

Scope and Sequence 5

Unit	Listening/Speaking **VIDEO**	Grammar **VIDEO**	Practical Skills	Pronunciation	Reading Skills
Welcome page 2	• Meet your classmates • Talk about your goals	• Review grammar terms • Review verb tenses			• Learn about your book
1 **Eva Gets the Job Done** page 5	• Make small talk with a coworker • Talk about what you would do if . . . • Discuss plans to achieve your goals	• Participial adjectives • Present unreal conditional; wish	• Reply to a business email	• Stress important words • Stress one of the syllables in words of more than one syllable	• Identify the main idea An article about the rule of thirds in photography
2 **Matt Finds a Way** page 19	• Talk about problems • Consider options • Make a decision	• Modals of obligation • Reported speech with modals	• Compare consumer ads	• Pronunciation of *have to = hafta* • Groups of consonant sounds	• Identify supporting details A web article about the Third Place
3 **Gary Helps Out** page 33	• Check on progress • Ask for advice • Identify needs	• Tag questions • Past perfect vs. past perfect continuous	• Compare invoice and purchase order	• Intonation in tag questions • Rising intonation in short questions to show interest or surprise	• Make connections between related information An article about stress management
4 **Kelly, the People Person** page 47	• Ask for help • Talk about interests and skills • Give instructions	• Object + infinitive after certain verbs • Noun clauses as objects	• Interpret a rental agreement	• Dropped vowels • Vowels pronounced like the names of vowel letters	• Paraphrase An article about national parks
5 **Eva's Challenging Day** page 61	• Troubleshoot a problem • Respond to criticism • Offer to help	• Modals: degrees of certainty • Adverb clauses: concession	• Evaluate marketing strategies	• Thought groups • Stress the most important word(s) in sentences or thought groups	• Understand sequence of events An article about roller coasters

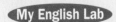
My English Lab

Vocabulary	Practical Skills	Writing	Unit Tests
Listening and Speaking	Grammar	Job-Seeking	Midterm Tests
Pronunciation	Reading		Final CASAS Test Prep

Writing Skills	Vocabulary ActiveTeach	Job-Seeking Skills	Career Pathways	CASAS Highlights	Common Core College and Career Readiness
• Write a biography • Use topic sentences	• Identify root words **Learning strategy:** • Use word webs Word list page 161	• Assess skills	• Develop interpersonal relationships • Sell an idea or product • Help others • Work as a team • Be self-aware	0.1.2, 0.1.3, 0.2.4, 1.3, 2.3.1, 4.1.9, 4.6, 4.8.1-4, 7.1, 7.2.4, 7.5.1	R.1, 2, 3, 4, 5, 6, 10 W.1, 2, 3, 4, 5, 7, 8 SL.1, 2, 3, 4, 5 L.1, 2, 3, 4, 5, 6, 7, 8
• Write about a problem and solutions • Use thesis statements in problem-and-solution essays	• Understand prefixes **Learning strategy:** • Learn words that go together Word list page 161	• Research jobs	• Communicate clearly • Sell an idea or product • Work as a team • Offer solutions • Make informed decisions • Organize	0.1.2, 0.1.3, 0.1.7, 1.2, 1.2.1, 1.3, 1.8, 1.9, 1.9.7, 4.1.3, 4.1.8, 4.6, 4.7.2, 4.8, 4.9, 7.2.3-4, 7.2.7, 7.3.1-4	R.1, 2, 3, 4, 5, 6, 10 W.1, 2, 3, 4, 5, 7, 8 SL.1, 2, 3, 4, 5, 8 L.1, 2, 3, 4, 5, 6, 7, 8
• Write a business letter • Follow business letter format	• Understand collocations **Learning strategy:** • Use familiar words or images to remember phrases Word list page 161	• Set goals	• Report on progress • Manage others • Deal with difficult decisions • Help others • Show concern • Give advice • Be self-aware • Offer solutions	0.1.2, 0.1.3, 0.1.8, 1.3, 1.6.3, 1.8, 4.1.9, 4.4, 4.4.5, 4.6.4, 4.8.2, 5.6.1, 7.1.1, 7.1.2, 7.2.3-4, 7.5.4, 7.5.5	R.1, 2, 3, 4, 5, 6, 10 W.1, 2, 3, 4, 5, 7, 8 SL.1, 2, 3, 4, 5 L.1, 2, 3, 4, 5, 6, 7, 8
• Write about cause and effect • Use logical connectors showing cause and effect	• Understand suffixes **Learning strategy:** • Write personal sentences Word list page 162	• Interpret employment ads	• Help others • Manage others • Communicate clearly • Promote yourself in an interview • Make informed decisions	0.1.2, 0.1.4, 0.1.7, 1.4.3, 1.4.5, 1.4.7, 2.7.3, 4.1, 4.1.2-3, 4.6.1, 4.7, 5.6.1-2, 7.1, 7.2.1, 7.3, 7.5.1	R.1, 2, 3, 4, 5, 6, 7, 8, 9, 10, 11, 12 W.1, 2, 3, 4, 5, 8 SL.1, 2, 3, 4, 5, 6 L.1, 2, 3, 4, 5, 6, 7, 8
• Write about steps in a process • Use time clauses to show order of steps	• Identify word families **Learning strategy:** • Group by function Word list page 162	• Write a cover letter	• Offer solutions • Manage others • Communicate a complaint • Manage your emotions • Learn from mistakes • Accept criticism • Help others • Show concern • Network	0.1.2, 0.1.3, 0.1.7, 2.5.8, 2.6.1, 4.1.2, 4.4, 4.5, 4.5.7, 4.6.1-4, 5.6.2, 7.2.3-4, 7.3, 7.5.3, 7.6.1, 7.7.2, 7.7.6	R.1, 2, 3, 4, 5, 6, 7, 9, 10 W.1, 2, 3, 4, 5, 7, 8 SL.1, 2, 3, 4, 5, 8 L.1, 2, 3, 4, 5, 6, 7, 8

For complete correlations please visit www.pearsoneltusa.com/projectsuccess

Scope and Sequence 5

Unit	Listening/Speaking **VIDEO**	Grammar **VIDEO**	Practical Skills	Pronunciation	Reading Skills
6 **Walt Has an Idea** page 75	• Propose an idea • Demonstrate technology skills • Compromise	• Adjective clauses • Passive voice with modals	• Interpret directions	• Stress in two-syllable nouns and verbs • /ð/ (*the*) and /θ/ (*think*)	• Identify author's purpose An article about Little Havana
7 **Matt Focuses on Safety** page 89	• Describe an accident • Identify unsafe working conditions • Talk about safety	• Reflexive pronouns • Past unreal conditional	• Interpret an accident report	• Linking in words that begin with vowel sounds • Unstressed vowel /ə/	• Make inferences A quiz about body language
8 **Walt Has an Opportunity** page 103	• Talk about time management • Ask for permission • Talk about travel plans	• Embedded questions with infinitives • Past modals	• Interpret a meeting agenda and minutes	• Linking in past modals • Pronunciation of *going to = gonna*	• Differentiate between fact and opinion A blog post about donating online
9 **Kelly Organizes an Event** page 117	• Convince someone • Organize teams • Justify a decision	• Future in the past • Causatives: *make, have, get*	• Interpret a workplace policy	• Pronunciation of *can* vs *can't* • Stress in compound nouns	• Summarize An article about pythons in the Everglades
10 **Gary Reviews the Situation** page 131	• Give constructive criticism • Talk about job advancement • Talk about success	• *Too / enough* + adjective + infinitive • The subjunctive	• Interpret a performance review	• Intonation to show strong feeling • *-ed* verb endings	• Interact with a text An interview with a food truck owner

 **My English Lab**

Vocabulary
Listening and Speaking
Pronunciation

Practical Skills
Grammar
Reading

Writing
Job-Seeking

Unit Tests
Midterm Tests
Final CASAS Test Prep

Writing Skills	Vocabulary ActiveTeach	Job-Seeking Skills	Career Pathways	CASAS Highlights	Common Core College and Career Readiness
• Write a description • Use sensory details	• Understand context clues **Learning strategy:** • Describe objects around you Word list page 162	• Prepare a resume	• Communicate clearly • Influence or persuade others • Sell an idea or product • Manage your emotions • Work as a team • Make informed decisions • Negotiate • Be self-aware	0.1.2, 0.1.3, 4.1.2, 4.5, 4.5.1, 4.5.6, 4.6, 7.2.4, 7.2.7, 7.3, 7.7.6	R.1, 2, 3, 4, 5, 6, 7, 8, 9, 10 W.1, 2, 3, 4, 5, 7, 8 SL.1, 2, 3, 4, 5 L.1, 2, 3, 4, 5, 6, 7, 8
• Write about unexpected consequences • Use expressions to introduce examples	• Understand idioms **Learning strategy:** • Learn words that have different meanings in different contexts Word list page 163	• Prepare for an interview	• Show concern • Manage others • Work as a team • Make informed decisions • Learn from mistakes • Report on progress • Offer solutions	0.1.2, 3.4, 3.4.2, 4.1.2, 4.3, 4.3.4, 4.4, 4.6, 4.6.5, 7.2.4	R.1, 2, 3, 4, 5, 6, 7, 9, 10, 11, 12 W.1, 2, 3, 4, 5, 7, 8 SL.1, 2, 3, 4, 5 L.1, 2, 3, 4, 5, 6, 7, 8
• Write a memo • Use appropriate tone	• Identify formal vs informal language **Learning strategy:** • Use vocabulary cards Word list page 163	• Interview, Part 1	• Manage stress • Prioritize tasks • Communicate a complaint • Develop interpersonal relationships • Promote yourself in an interview	0.1.2, 2.2.3-5, 4.1.5, 4.1.7, 4.2, 4.6, 4.6.2-3, 7.1.4, 7.2.3-4, 7.5	R.1, 2, 3, 4, 5, 6, 7, 9, 10, 11, 12 W.1, 2, 3, 4, 5, 7, 8 SL.1, 2, 3, 4, 5 L.1, 2, 3, 4, 5, 6, 7, 8
• Write a statement of opinion • Use persuasive language	• Understand connotations **Learning strategy:** • Use prefixes Word list page 163	• Interview, Part 2	• Influence or persuade others • Organize • Work as a team • Manage your emotions • Navigate office politics • Promote yourself in an interview	0.1.3, 0.1.7, 3.5.9, 4.1.5, 4.1.7, 4.2, 4.2.4, 4.6, 4.7, 4.8.1, 5.6.2, 5.7.1-2, 7.3, 7.4.2	R.1, 2, 3, 4, 5, 6, 7, 9, 10, 11, 12 W.1, 2, 3, 4, 5, 7, 8 SL.1, 2, 3, 4, 5 L.1, 2, 3, 4, 5, 6, 7, 8
• Write a self-evaluation • Use expressions to signal contrast	• Understand figurative language **Learning strategy:** • Group by positive or negative meanings Word list page 164	• Write a thank you message	• Manage others • Communicate a complaint • Show tact • Demonstrate resilience • Accept criticism • Develop interpersonal relationships	0.1.2, 4.1.6, 4.1.7, 4.4, 4.4.2-4, 4.6.1, 7.1, 7.2.3-4, 7.7.2	R.1, 2, 3, 4, 5, 6, 7, 8, 9, 10, 11, 12 W.1, 2, 3, 4, 5, 7, 8 SL.1, 2, 3, 4, 5 L.1, 2, 3, 4, 5, 6, 7, 8

Project Success is a dynamic six-level, four-skills multimedia course for adults and young adults. It offers a comprehensive and integrated program for false-beginner to low-advanced learners, with a classroom and online curriculum correlated to national and state standards.

KEY FEATURES

In developing this course we focused on our students' future aspirations, and on their current realities. Through inspiring stories of adults working and mastering life's challenges, we illustrate the skills and competencies adult English language learners need to participate fully and progress in their roles at home, work, school, and in the community. To create versatile and dynamic learning tools, we integrate digital features such as video, audio, and an online curriculum into one unified and comprehensive course. The result is *Project Success*: the first blended digital course designed for adult-education English language learners.

MULTIMEDIA: INSIDE AND OUTSIDE THE CLASSROOM

All *Project Success* materials are technologically integrated for seamless independent and classroom learning. The user-friendly digital interface will appeal to students who are already technologically adept, while providing full support for students who have less computer experience.

In class, the teacher uses the **ActiveTeach** DVD-ROM to project the lessons on the board. Video, audio, flashcards, conversation frameworks, checklists, comprehension questions, and other learning material are all available at the click of a button. Students use their print **Student Book** as they participate in class activities, take notes, and interact in group work.

Outside of class, students access their Project Success **eText** to review the videos, audio, and eFlashcards from class. They use their **MyEnglishLab** access code to get further practice online with new listenings and readings, additional practice activities, and video-based exercises.

A VARIETY OF WORKFORCE AND LIFE SKILLS

Each level of *Project Success* presents a different cast of characters at a different workplace. In each book, students learn instrumental language, employment, and educational skills as they watch the characters interact with co-workers, customers, family, and friends. As students move through the series, level by level, they learn about six important sectors in today's economy: food service, hospitality, healthcare, higher education, business, and retail.

The language and skills involved in daily life range from following directions, to phone conversations, to helping customers, to asking permission to leave early. By representing a day in the life of a character, *Project Success* can introduce a diverse sampling of the content, language, and competencies involved in daily life and work. This approach allows students to learn diverse competencies and then practice them, in different settings and contexts, at different points in the curriculum.

VIDEO VIGNETTES

Each unit is organized around a series of short videos that follow one main character through his or her workday. In Listening and Speaking lessons, students watch the video together, see the character model a key competency in a realistic setting, and then practice the competency in pairs and groups. Discussion questions and group activities encourage students to identify and interpret the rich cultural content embedded in the video. The unit's grammar points are presented in the context of natural language in the video and then highlighted for more study and practice in a separate grammar lesson.

CRITICAL THINKING SKILLS

In the *What do you think?* activity at the end of nearly every lesson, students analyze, evaluate, infer, or relate content in the lesson to other contexts and situations.

A ROBUST ASSESSMENT STRAND

The series includes a rich assessment package that consists of unit review tests, midterms, and a CASAS-like final test. The tests assess students on CASAS objectives which are integrated into practical skills and listening strands.

The tests are available online or in a printable version on the ActiveTeach.

THE COMPONENTS:

ActiveTeach

This is a powerful digital platform for teachers. It blends a digital form of the Student Book with interactive whiteboard (IWB) software and printable support materials.

MyEnglishLab

This is a dynamic, easy-to-use online learning and assessment program that is integral to the *Project Success* curriculum. Original interactive activities extend student practice of vocabulary, listening, speaking, pronunciation, grammar, reading, writing, and practical skills from the classroom learning component.

eText

The eText is a digital version of the Student Book with all the audio and video integrated, and with a complete set of the pop-up eFlashcards.

To the Student

WELCOME TO *PROJECT SUCCESS*!

Project Success is a six-level digital and print English program designed for you. It teaches English, employment, and learning skills for your success at work and school.

YOUR CLASSROOM LEARNING

Bring the Student Book to your classroom to learn new material and to practice with your classmates in groups. Every unit has:

- Three video-based lessons for your listening and speaking skills
- One practical skills lesson
- Two grammar lessons
- One lesson for getting a job
- One lesson for writing
- One lesson for reading
- One review page

YOUR ONLINE LEARNING

Your access code is on the front cover of your Student Book. Use the access code to go online. There you will find eText and MyEnglishLab.

Go to your eText to review what you learned in class. You can watch the videos again, listen to audio, and review the Vocabulary Flashcards.

Go to MyEnglishLab online to practice what you learned in class. MyEnglishLab has:

- Extra listening practice
- Extra reading practice
- Extra grammar practice
- Extra writing practice
- Extra practice of vocabulary skills
- Extra practice of practical skills
- Additional video-based exercises
- "Record and compare," so you can record yourself and listen to your own pronunciation
- Instant feedback
- Job-seeking activities

Welcome Unit

MEET YOUR CLASSMATES

A **PAIRS** Introduce yourself to your partner.

B **PAIRS** Interview your partner. Take notes.

1. Where are you from? _____
2. When did you come to the United States? _____
3. Do you have a family? _____
4. What do you like to do on the weekend? _____
5. What kinds of food do you like? _____
6. Do you have any special skills or talents? _____
7. How long have you been a student at this school? _____
8. Why are you studying English? _____
9. What will you do when you finish this class? _____
10. Do you work? What do you do? _____

C Introduce your partner to the class. Give your partner's name and say one or two things you learned about him/her.

This is Jorge Medina. He's from Mexico. He came to the United States five years ago . . .

TALK ABOUT YOUR GOALS

A Think about your goals. What do you want to achieve in your personal/family life, your work life, and your education? Complete the chart.

	In Three Months	In One Year	In Five Years
My personal/ family goals			
My work goals			
My educational goals			

B **PAIRS** Choose two of your most important goals from Exercise A. Talk about your goals with a partner. Include the following questions in your discussion.

1. Why do you want to achieve your goal?
2. What skills do you need to learn before you can achieve it?
3. What might get in the way of your goal?
4. How long will it take for you to achieve your goal?

REVIEW GRAMMAR TERMS

PAIRS Read the definitions. Complete them with the parts of speech from the box.

adjective   adverb   noun   preposition   pronoun   ~~verb~~

1. ___verb___ = a word or group of words that describes an action, experience, or state of being; example: *work*

2. _____ = a word or group or words that represents a person, place, thing, quality, action, or idea; example: *teacher*

3. _____ = a word that describes or adds to the meaning of a verb, adjective, another adverb, or a sentence; example: *slowly*

4. _____ = a word that is used instead of a noun; example: *he*

5. _____ = a word that describes a noun or pronoun; example: *new*

6. _____ = a word or group or words that is used before a noun or pronoun to show place, time, direction; example: *in*

REVIEW VERB FORMS

PAIRS Identify the underlined parts of the sentences. Use the verb forms from the box.

future   gerund   past perfect   present perfect
present continuous   ~~simple present~~   simple past

1. I <u>live</u> in Miami, Florida.   ___simple present___

2. I <u>went</u> to Colombia last year.   _____

3. I enjoy <u>playing</u> soccer.   _____

4. I'm <u>going to enroll</u> in a nursing program soon.   _____

5. I'm <u>studying</u> English right now.   _____

6. I <u>have studied</u> English for five years.   _____

7. I <u>had studied</u> English in China before I moved here. _____

LEARN ABOUT *PROJECT SUCCESS*

A **Learn about your book.**
1. Look at the cover of your book. What's the title?
2. Look at the inside front cover. Find the access code.
3. <u>See page iii.</u> How many units are in your book?
4. Where can you find a list of vocabulary words?

B **Meet the characters in your book.**
They all work at Traven Global Coffee.

I'm Eva Vera. I'm a sales manager here at Traven Global Coffee in Miami, Florida. I love coffee . . . and I love my job.

I'm Matt Molino. I manage the Traven Global warehouse. I'm married, and I have two kids . . . and I love fishing!

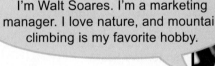

I'm Walt Soares. I'm a marketing manager. I love nature, and mountain climbing is my favorite hobby.

I'm Gary Frye. I'm the operations manager here at Traven Global, so I have a lot of staff to supervise. I've worked at this company for over 20 years.

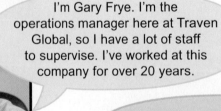

I'm Kelly Chen. I'm a human resources manager. I enjoy working with people and figuring out ways that our company can help the Miami community.

1 Eva Gets the Job Done

MY GOALS

- ☐ Make small talk with a coworker
- ☐ Reply to a business email
- ☐ Talk about what you would do if . . .
- ☐ Discuss plans to achieve your goals
- ☐ Assess skills

Go to MyEnglishLab for more practice after each lesson.

Eva Vera

Eva   *Today*
A big new hotel loves our coffee! Have I found another new customer for Traven Global . . . ?

1

Make small talk with a coworker

GET READY TO WATCH

Eva Vera and Matt Molino work at a coffee company called Traven Global Coffee. Where do you think they are, and what can you say about them?

WATCH

A ◼◀ Watch the video. Were your guesses correct?

B ◼◀ Watch the video again. Answer the questions.

1. What did Matt do last weekend?

2. What did Eva do last weekend?

3. Why is Eva busy?

4. What does Matt want Eva to do?

CONVERSATION

A ◼◀ Watch part of the video. Complete the conversation.

Eva: How was your weekend?

Matt: It was a lot of fun. I went fishing with my son, and he caught a big _____!

Eva: Wow! I'll bet he was really excited!

Matt: I was, too! . . . How about you? What did you do last weekend?

Eva: Well, on Saturday, I went to the _____ with my daughters. We went swimming, and I took some photos.

Matt: Sounds like fun. You're really into photography, aren't you?

Eva: Yes, I am. I take my camera with me wherever I go. I got an interesting _____ of the sunset on Saturday. . . . Here, you want to see it?

Matt: Wow! What an amazing picture! I love it!

B PAIRS Practice the conversation.

C Read the conversation again. Underline two "small talk" questions about a coworker's personal life.

D PAIRS Have similar conversations. Talk about your personal life.

> ### Pronunciation Note
>
> Important words are stressed. We make them longer and louder. We usually stress words that have a clear meaning.
>
> ◀))) **Listen and repeat.**
>
> I went **fishing** with my **son**.
>
> I'll bet he was **really excited**!

> ### Note
>
> **MAKE SMALL TALK**
> When you make small talk with a coworker, you ask and answer questions about your personal life. When you make small talk with a stranger, you talk about "safe" topics only, such as the weather.

WHAT DO YOU THINK?

PAIRS In the video, how does Eva end the conversation? What else could she have said or done to end it?

GRAMMAR

② Participial adjectives

STUDY Participial Adjectives

-ing	-ed
Photography is an **interest**ing hobby.	Eva is **interest**ed in photography.
Eva is an **amaz**ing photographer.	Matt was **amaz**ed by Eva's pictures.
The park is a **relax**ing place.	I feel **relax**ed in the park.

Grammar Note

- Participial adjectives are formed from verbs.
- Adjectives ending in *-ing* are present participles. They describe the cause of a feeling.
- Adjectives ending in *-ed* are past participles. They describe how a person feels.
- The preposition *by* often follows *-ed* adjectives: *Mike was amazed by Eva's pictures.*

See page 155 for a list of participial adjectives.

PRACTICE

 A **Circle the correct adjectives.**

If you're (1) (bored)/ boring on the weekends, take up a hobby or sport. Try to choose an
(2) **entertaining / entertained** activity. For example, you might be (3) **fascinated / fascinating**
by digital photography. Perhaps cooking is a more (4) **satisfied / satisfying** hobby. Or perhaps
you like (5) **excited / exciting** sports such as surfing. The important thing is to choose
something that you are (6) **interested / interesting** in.

B **Complete the paragraph. Use the -ed or -ing forms of the verbs.**

Eva goes to the beach as often as she can. She is very ____*stimulated*____ by the
                                                    1. stimulate

beach because there are so many _____ things to photograph there. She
                                      2. interest

has photographed _____ sunsets and people from all over the world.
                      3. amaze

She has even photographed _____ tropical storms! Eva is unusual. Most
                                4. thrill

people enjoy going to the beach just to relax. Whenever they feel _____,
                                                                    5. exhaust

or they are _____ by their jobs, they go to the beach to have some fun.
              6. frustrate

WHAT ABOUT YOU?

GROUPS Ask and answer questions about your feelings. Ask, *When do you feel ____ed?*
What is ____ing for you? Use the words from the box and other participial adjectives.

(bored   boring   frustrated   frustrating   relaxed   relaxing)

3 Reply to a business email

GET READY

Eva is having a business email exchange with Rob Fisher. What are some differences between business emails and social emails?

PRACTICAL READING

A **Scan (read quickly) the two emails. Who is Rob Fisher?**

From: Robert Fisher (rfisher@hotelelypso.com)
Sent: Tuesday, February 2, 2014, 10:15 A.M.
To: Eva Vera (evera@tgc.com)
Subject: Sweet Canopy blend

Hello, Eva,

It was a pleasure meeting you yesterday to discuss coffee choices for our convention guests. Thank you for the opportunity to taste some of your coffees.

As you know, we're looking for an organic gourmet blend that is reasonably priced. I liked the Brava Blend, but I preferred your new blend, Sweet Canopy. I think it could be a good fit for us. Could you get me a price quote and marketing materials for the blend as soon as possible? We're hosting a couple of big conventions next month, so we need to make a decision quickly.

Thank you.

Regards,
Rob

Robert Fisher
Food and Beverage Manager
Hotel Elypso
The South Beach Hotel of Choice

From: Eva Vera (evera@tgc.com)
Sent: Tuesday, February 2, 2014, 11:00 A.M.
To: Robert Fisher (rfisher@hotelelypso.com)
Subject: Re: Sweet Canopy blend
Attachment: price_quote.doc

Hi, Rob,

Yes, it was a pleasure meeting you. I'm excited that you're interested in Sweet Canopy. I think your convention guests will love the blend!

As requested, I'm attaching a price quote for Sweet Canopy. As for the marketing materials, my goal is to get those to you later today.

Best regards,
Eva

Eva Vera
Sales Manager
Traven Global Coffee
3818 N. Miami Ave.
Miami, FL 33127

B Circle the correct words from the emails.

1. Hector sent the customer the document in **an attachment** / **a convention** to his email.

2. When I saw the company's **beverage** / **price quote** for the product, I decided it was too expensive.

3. I'm going to attend a **convention** / **host** for toy manufacturers.

4. Companies often include beautiful photographs in their **marketing materials** / **price quotes** for products.

5. The Petersons own **an organic** / **a gourmet** farm, so they don't use any chemicals or pesticides on their crops.

C Read the first email again. Circle the correct answers.

1. What is the relationship between Eva and Rob Fisher?
   a. salesperson and customer   **b.** hotel manager and convention guest

2. What type of coffee blend is Rob interested in?
   a. a very expensive organic blend   **b.** a cheaper gourmet blend

3. What does Rob want Eva to get for him?
   a. a price quote and coffee blends   **b.** a price quote and marketing materials

4. What does Rob need to choose quickly?
   a. a convention to host   **b.** a coffee to serve at his conventions

D Read the second email again. Answer the questions.

1. What time does Eva reply to Rob's email?

2. How long does it take for Eva to reply to Rob's email?

3. What does Eva send to Rob as an attachment?

4. What is Eva going to deliver to Rob later?

PRACTICAL LISTENING

◄))) Listen to the podcast about customer service and emails. Answer the questions.

1. Why are emails important for businesses?

2. What should you do when you first receive a business email?

3. When should you reply to an email?

4. How should business emails sound?

5. After you've written your reply, what should you do before you send it?

WHAT DO YOU THINK?

GROUPS Review the email exchange and the podcast. Discuss. Did Eva reply appropriately to Rob's email? Give reasons for your answer.

LISTENING AND SPEAKING

Talk about what you would do if . . .

GET READY TO WATCH

Eva and Walt Soares are chatting in the break room. Do you talk to your coworkers on break? What do you usually talk about?

WATCH

■◀ **Watch the video. Answer the questions.**

1. Where did Eva read about Walt?
2. What does Walt love to do?
3. Where does Eva want to go?
4. What is Walt going to try to do for Eva?

CONVERSATION

A ■◀ **Watch part of the video. Complete the conversation.**

Eva: If you were rich, would you really _____ all the highest mountains in the world?

Walt: Yes, I would. I climb mountains every chance I get!

Eva: Really? Which ones have you climbed?

Walt: Well, so far, the highest one I've climbed is Mount Whitney in California.

It was an awesome _____! . . .

Eva: Wow!

Walt: So what would you do if you had a lot of time and money?

Eva: I would visit some of the _coffe producing_ countries. . . . Guatemala, Kenya . . . .

Walt: Oh, interesting!

B PAIRS **Practice the conversation.**

C **Read the conversation again. Underline the things Walt and Eva would do if they had a lot of time and money.**

D PAIRS **Have similar conversations. What would you do if you had a lot of time and money? Begin your answers, _I would_ . . .**

WHAT DO YOU THINK?

PAIRS Compare Eva's wishful thinking in the video with Walt's. Whose do you think sounds more fun or interesting? Why?

STUDY **Present Unreal Conditional; *wish***

Present Unreal Conditional

If clause	Result clause
If Eva **had** more time,	she **would** travel.
If you **were** rich,	**would** you buy a big house?
If there **were** a mountain here,	we **could** climb it.

Wishes About Present/Future Situations

I **wish** I **knew** how to take good photos.
She **wishes** she **were** good at singing.
Does he **wish** he **could** ski?

Grammar Note

· Use present unreal conditional sentences to talk about things that are untrue or impossible.
· The *if* clause can begin or end a sentence. If it ends the sentence, don't use a comma:
  Eva ***would*** *travel if she* ***had*** *more time.*
· Use *wish* + simple past when you want reality to be different or the opposite of the true situation.

PRACTICE

A **Read Eva's blog. Circle the correct forms. Use the present unreal conditional or *wish* and the simple past.**

I wish I (1) **can** / (could) play a musical instrument. If I (2) **have** / **had** more time, I (3) **will** / **would** learn to play the flute. I (4) **will** / **would** learn to play well if I (5) **practice** / **practiced** a lot. If I (6) **was** / **were** really talented, I (7) **can** / **could** perform in front of other people. If people (8) **enjoy** / **enjoyed** watching me perform, I (9) **can** / **could** become a world-famous professional musician. . . . Well, I can dream, can't I?

B **Complete the sentences. Use the present unreal conditional or *wish* and the simple past of the verbs.**

1. If you ___took___ time off, what ___would___ you do?
    _{take}   _{will}

2. _____ you try mountain climbing if you _____ the opportunity?
    _{will}   _{have}

3. If you _____ on a trip, where _____ you go?
    _{go}   _{will}

4. I wish I _____ Chinese. If you _____ learn another language, what _____ it be?
    _{know}   _{can}   _{will}

5. My friend wishes he _____ a rock star. What do you wish you _____ do or be?
    _{be}   _{can}

WHAT ABOUT YOU?

PAIRS Ask and answer the questions in Exercise B.

6

Identify the main idea

GET READY

On her break, Eva is reading an article about photography. Do you like to take photos?

READ

◀⦂)) **Listen and read the article on page 13. What does the author suggest readers do to make their photographs more interesting?**

AFTER YOU READ

A **Read the Reading Skill. Read the article again. Underline the main idea statement.**

Reading Skill

The **main idea** of an article is the most important point the writer is trying to make. Often, the writer states the main idea clearly, but sometimes you will have to put the main idea into your own words. If there is a main idea statement, it usually appears in the first paragraph of the article, but not always.

B **PAIRS** **Do these photos follow the rule of thirds? Why or why not? Explain.**

VOCABULARY STUDY Roots

Build Your Vocabulary

A **root** is the most basic part of a word. Sometimes, English words come from Greek and Latin roots. For example, *dentist* comes from the Latin root *dent*, which means "tooth." Learning roots can help you understand new words.

Read the Build Your Vocabulary note. Then read the chart. For each root, find one more example of a word with the same root in the article.

Root	Meaning	Example	Example from Article
photo	light	photograph	
imag	picture, likeness	imagine (= to form a picture in the mind)	
vi / vis	see	visible	

WHAT DO YOU THINK?

GROUPS Discuss. Can you think of any other ways besides the rule of thirds to make a photo interesting?

ON THE WEB

For more information, go online and search "photography tips." Find one more helpful tip. Report back to the class.

The Rule of Thirds

You just got back from a wedding. You eagerly show your family the photos you took . . . but most of them are downright bad. Why does this always happen? How can you take photos that people will enjoy looking at? It's time for you to learn a basic rule of composition that many artists and photographers use to make their images more interesting—the rule of thirds.

Photo 1

How does the rule of thirds work? Let's start by taking a look at a couple of photos—Photos 1 and 2. Which do you think is better, and why?

Most people would say that the second photo is better than the first. In Photo 1, the hut is right in the center of the picture. This makes the photo kind of boring. Photo 2, on the other hand, follows the rule of thirds. Figure 1 illustrates how it does this.

Photo 2

The rectangular grid over the photo has two vertical lines and two horizontal lines. They divide the picture into thirds. Pay attention to the intersections of the four lines. Try to place your photo's subject(s) somewhere near these four intersections. You can also place them along the lines. Notice how the subject of Photo 2, the hut, is not in the center of the photograph. It is positioned at the intersection of the right vertical line and the horizontal line.

Figure 1

Now let's apply the rule of thirds to another pair of photos. In Photo 3, the horizon runs across the middle of the photo. It cuts the photo into two halves. In Photo 4, however, the horizon lies along the bottom horizontal line. The bright sun attracts the eye near the top horizontal line. The result: a more interesting and

Photo 3

Photo 4

appealing photo than Photo 3. Lesson to be learned: Try not to put the horizon in the middle of your picture!

You may think the rule of thirds sounds too complicated for you to follow. But it really isn't, especially with today's digital cameras. Just select the rule of thirds feature. The rectangular grid will appear when you look through the viewfinder.

So the next time you take a photo, don't just snap a quick shot of someone standing right in the center of the frame. Instead, use the rule of thirds to think about where you should position the subjects of your photos . . . and take your photographs to a whole new level!

7

Write a biography

 GET READY

Traven Global Coffee's website features employee bios. Eva is reading her bio.
Have you ever had to write a bio of yourself or someone else?

 STUDY THE MODEL

A **Read part of Eva's bio. Why do you think companies post employee bios on their websites?**

Meet Eva Vera, Sales Manager

Since the beginning of her career, Eva Vera has worked with coffee. At her first job, she answered the phones at a beverage company. Next, she worked at a coffee shop in downtown Miami. There she mastered the art of making all kinds of fancy coffee drinks. She also learned about different kinds of coffee from around the world. Eva realized that she wanted to find out more about the coffee industry. So she joined Traven Global Coffee as a sales representative. Soon she was promoted to sales manager. Her job responsibilities include directing the sales team and setting sales goals. She also helps her staff to build relationships with customers and land new accounts.

Eva is a strong believer in education. First, she earned an associate's degree in business administration from Miami-Dade Community College. In 2005, she received a bachelor's degree in international business from the University of Miami. She recently enrolled in an MBA program there.

Eva has an international background. She was born on a farm in Lima, Peru. She is fluent in Spanish. She moved to this country when she was six years old. She was raised in Fort Lauderdale. She moved to Miami to go to college and decided to stay.

Outside of work, Eva has many interests and hobbies. She loves to travel. She swims for exercise, sometimes at the beach. She is very good at digital photography. Most importantly, she spends as much time as she can with her two daughters.

Writing Tip

The **topic sentence** tells the main idea of a paragraph. Each paragraph has its own topic sentence. The topic sentence is often the first sentence in the paragraph, but not always. All the other sentences in the paragraph should give more information about the topic sentence.

B **Read the Writing Tip. Then read Eva's bio again. Underline the topic sentence for each paragraph.**

C Look at the chart the writer used and complete it with information from the Model.

Work History	Education	Background	Interests, Hobbies
1.	1.	1. Born in Lima, Peru	1. Travel
2. Worked at coffee shop	2.	2.	2.
3. Sales representative, Traven Global Coffee	3.	3.	3.
4.		4.	4.

BEFORE YOU WRITE

You're going to write a biography of yourself or a friend or family member. If you write about yourself, use the third person (*he/she*). Complete the chart below to plan your writing. Use a separate piece of paper if necessary.

Work History	Education	Background	Interests, Hobbies

WRITE

Write your biography. Review the Model and the Writing Tip. Use the ideas in your chart. Use a separate piece of paper.

LISTENING AND SPEAKING

8

Discuss plans to achieve your goals

GET READY TO WATCH

Eva and Walt are having a meeting.
What do you think they are looking at?

WATCH

A ◼◀ Watch the video.
Was your guess correct?

B ◼◀ Watch the video again. Answer the questions.

1. What does Eva plan to do with the materials Walt is showing her?

2. What does Eva think she will have to offer Rob Fisher?

3. What is Eva going to bring with her to the hotel?

4. Why does Eva call Walt at the end of the video?

CONVERSATION

A ◼◀ Watch part of the video.
Complete the conversation.

Walt: So what's your next step?

Eva: Well, Rob is waiting to see these marketing materials. So I'm going to head over there right after this.

Walt: And you already sent him a price quote, right?

Eva: Yes, but I know he's going to want to
_____ the price.

Walt: Why? What did he say?

Eva: He mentioned that he's looking for a "reasonably priced" blend.

So I'm pretty sure I'm going to have to offer him a big _____.

Walt: Yeah, you're probably right. You should bring a gift basket with you, too.

That always makes a good _____.

Eva: Uh-huh. I'm going to pick one up in the warehouse.

B PAIRS **Practice the conversation.**

C **Read the conversation again. Underline the parts where Eva discusses her plan for landing the Hotel Elypso account.**

D PAIRS **Think of a goal that you want to achieve and make a plan to achieve it. Then have your own conversations about the steps you plan to take to achieve your goals.**

Pronunciation Note

In words with more than one syllable, one of the syllables is stressed. The vowel sound is long and clear.

◀)) **Listen and repeat. Notice where we put the stress in words that end in -ate.**

dis·count   fan·**tas**·tic

ma·**te**·ri·als   **rea**·son·a·bly

ne·**go**·ti·ate   ap·**pro**·pri·ate

WHAT DO YOU THINK?

GROUPS In the video, Eva's plan is successful. Can you think of other situations in which people made plans to achieve goals? Were their plans successful? Why or why not?

JOB-SEEKING SKILLS
Assess skills

Sal Morales *Today*
I've been an accountant at Julio's for 5 years. It's been fun, but it's time to look for a new job.

GET READY

Sal is Eva's friend. He's going to start looking for a new job soon. What are some things people think about when they decide to look for a new job?

IDENTIFY JOB SKILLS

A **Sal completed a job skills assessment list. Read how he rated himself. Then answer the questions.**

Rating Key: 0 = do not have skill   2 = have skill
            1 = have skill but need to improve   3 = am very good at skill

Basic Skills	Rating
I like to learn to new things.	2
I am good at math. I like to work with numbers.	3
I am a good listener. When others talk, I pay attention.	3
I am a good writer.	2
I am a good public speaker. I enjoy speaking in front of people.	0
Critical Thinking	
When I have a problem, I can think about it and find solutions.	3
Personal Qualities	
I am confident. I take the initiative.	2
I am responsible. I set goals and achieve them.	3
Managing Resources and Information	
I manage money well. I don't spend more money than I make.	3
I am organized. I keep files in order. I can find information quickly.	3
I see the big picture. I can prioritize projects and get things done.	3
Social Skills	
I get along with people of different backgrounds and experiences.	3
I am a natural leader. I like to guide other people.	0
I like helping other people.	2
Technology	
I like to use computers and other technology.	2
I can fix problems with computers and other technology.	0

1. Which kinds of skills in the list are about dealing with other people?

2. Which kinds of skills in the list are about working alone to solve problems?

3. Which kinds of skills is Sal good at?

4. Which specific skills does Sal need to improve?

B **PAIRS How would you describe Sal? What kinds of jobs do you think he might be good at?**

PUT YOUR IDEAS TO WORK

A See page 157 for a job skills assessment list. **Complete the list. Give yourself a rating from 0 to 3 for each skill.**

B **PAIRS Discuss your skills with your partner. Which skills are you confident about? Which skills do you want to learn or improve? How can you learn new skills or improve the skills you have?**

GRAMMAR

See page 145 for your Grammar Review.

VOCABULARY See page 161 for the Unit 1 Vocabulary.

Vocabulary Learning Strategy: Use Word Webs

A Make word webs with the words on the list. Add additional words to the webs below. Use a separate piece of paper.

B Circle 5 words in Exercise A. Write a sentence for each word.

SPELLING See page 161 for the Unit 1 Vocabulary.

CLASS Choose 10 words for a spelling test.

LISTENING PLUS

Watch each video. Write the story of Eva's day on a separate piece of paper.

> Eva makes small talk with a coworker. His name is Matt. She tells him that she went to the beach and took photos last weekend. . . .

NOW I CAN

PAIRS See page 5 for the Unit 1 Goals. Check ☑ the things you can do. Underline the things you want to study more. Then share your information with a partner.

> I can _____. I need more practice with _____.

2 Matt Finds a Way

MY GOALS

- [ ] Talk about problems
- [ ] Compare consumer ads
- [ ] Consider options
- [ ] Make a decision
- [ ] Research jobs

Go to MyEnglishLab for more practice after each lesson.

Matt Molino
Matt   *Today*
I'm planning to leave work early to go fishing. I hope there are no last-minute problems.

LISTENING AND SPEAKING

1

Talk about problems

GET READY TO WATCH

Matt was planning to leave work early, but he can't because his boss Gary Frye wants to talk to him. Have you ever had to stay late at work? Why?

WATCH

■◀ **Watch the video. Answer the questions.**

1. Why does Gary want to buy more coffee beans?
2. What problems does Matt bring up?
3. What does Gary want Matt to do before they buy the coffee?
4. What does Gary say he will do before meeting Matt again?

CONVERSATION

A ■◀ **Watch part of the video. Complete the conversation.**

Gary: Lucas thinks we should buy now or we'll miss out.

So do I. This could be a great _____ for us.

Matt: It could be, but . . .

Gary: But, what?

Matt: I'm worried that we don't have enough warehouse

space for a lot more _____.

Gary: Hmm. That could be a problem. The warehouse is already pretty full.

Matt: I have another _____, too. What if we can't sell all this new inventory?

Gary: Another good point. Obviously, we have to make sure we don't get stuck with a whole lot of unsold coffee beans!

> **Pronunciation Note**
>
> The word *have* usually ends with the sound /v/, but in conversation, we often pronounce *have to* as "hafta," with the sound /f/.
>
> ◀)) **Listen and repeat.**
>
> I have another concern.
>
> We have to (= "hafta") make sure.
>
> We don't have to (= "hafta") make a move on this.

B PAIRS **Practice the conversation.**

C **Read the conversation again. Underline two problems Matt brings up when he hears Gary's plan.**

D PAIRS **Think about plans for improving your school and make a list of possible problems with the plans. Then have your own conversations. Switch roles.**

Student A: Suggest a plan to improve your school.

Student B: Point out problems you see with the plan.

WHAT DO YOU THINK?

GROUPS In the video, Matt points out problems with Gary's plan. Should an employee point out problems with a supervisor's plan? Why or why not?

2 Modals of obligation

STUDY Modals of Obligation

Subject	Modal	Base Form of Verb	
New employees	must	report	to Human Resources.
Customers	must not	use	the employee bathroom.
Karla and Mia	have to	finish	the project by Friday.
Mike	doesn't have to	make	a decision quickly.
Does Sonia	have to	watch	the training video today?
Gary	had to	leave	early yesterday.

Grammar Note

- Use *must* and *have to* to show that something is necessary.
- *Must* is more common in formal, written English. *Have to* is more common in conversations.
- Use *must not* to show that something is not allowed. Do not use *mustn't* in American English.
- Use *don't/doesn't have to* to show that something is not necessary.
- Use *had to* for both *must* and *have to* in the past.

PRACTICE

A **Circle the correct words.**

1. All new employees (must) / don't have to fill out a W-2 tax form.

2. I must / had to check inventory at the store all last week.

3. Do you have to / must work on weekends?

4. She doesn't have to / must not work late. She can finish that tomorrow.

5. I know there are empty spots in our employee parking lot, but you aren't an
   employee, so you must not / don't have to park your car there.

B **Complete the conversation. Use the words from the box.**

(don't have to   had to   have to   must   must not)

A: Do I (1) _____ *have to* _____ wear a red shirt and black pants at work?

B: Well, you (2) _____ wear a red T-shirt, but you (3) _____
wear black pants. You can wear jeans.

A: Cool. What time do I (4) _____ start work?

B: At 10 A.M. Please be on time. This is from our employee handbook: "Employees

(5) _____ be late for work. If an employee is late, he/she

(6) _____ report to the shift manager." Last week, I

(7) _____ fire someone for being late too many times.

WHAT ABOUT YOU?

PAIRS Talk about 4 things you *have to* or *must* do at work or school. What rules do you have
to follow? Then talk about 3 things you don't have to do.

3 Compare consumer ads

GET READY

Matt wants to buy a new car. He is reading car ads. Have you ever bought a car? How did you find the car you bought?

PRACTICAL READING

A **Scan the newspaper ad and the online ad. What kind of car is featured in both ads?**

CRUISE MODITA

Nationwide Clearance Event!

NEW 2014 Modita Galley LE

$23,983

Retail price
$26,360

Automatic, air-conditioning, low fuel emissions, cruise control, 2-year complimentary maintenance plan, includes $2,377 Cruise Modita discount.

CONTACT US TODAY!
cruisemodita.com
Cruise Modita • 55 NW 158th Ave, Miami
(305) 555-5656

HOME | NEW CARS | USED CARS | SPECIALS | SERVICE | PARTS

MIAMI MODITA

Sales: (305) 555-2534

2013 Modita Galley LE
Retail Price: $24,975
Internet Price: $16,991
You Save: $7,984!!

PREOWNED VEHICLE PRICED TO SELL!

Body style: sedan
VIN: 4T1BF3EK1BU132470
Mileage: 18,550

Check out this outstanding 2013 Modita Galley!
This car is equipped with features such as Air-conditioning, 6 Speakers, AM/FM radio, CD player, Delay-off headlights, Driver vanity mirror, and Front-impact airbags.

B Read the ads more carefully. Complete the sentences. Use the words from the box.

> clearance event   complimentary   maintenance   mileage
> preowned   retail price   VIN

1. I bought a _____ car because it was cheaper than a new car.
2. That car has very low _____—it's only been driven 5,000 miles.
3. The dealership lowered its prices a lot for its annual _____.
4. The _____ of that car is $30,100, but we're offering it for $28,100.
5. The car is making a funny sound, so we should take it in for _____.
6. If you know the _____ of a used car, you can look it up on the Internet and see if it's been in any accidents.
7. The salesperson offered me a _____ gift card if I took the car for a test drive.

C Read the ads again. Check [✓] the correct columns in the chart.

Which dealership . . .	Cruise Modita	Miami Modita
1. is located in Miami?		
2. is offering a used car?		
3. offers free maintenance for two years?		
4. offers a $2,377 discount?		
5. offers cars with air-conditioning?		

D PAIRS Look at the ads again. Which car would you buy? Why? Think about price, features, and age of the car.

PRACTICAL LISTENING

🔊)) Listen to the radio ad. Answer the questions.

1. What is happening today?
2. What features does the car in the ad have?
3. How much did the woman pay for her car?
4. Why does the woman think Parker Modita is awesome?
5. Where is Parker Modita located?
6. How can people contact Parker Modita?

WHAT DO YOU THINK?

GROUPS Which ad do you think is most effective at persuading customers to check out the cars it is offering: the newspaper ad, the online ad, or the radio ad?
Give reasons for your answers.

LISTENING AND SPEAKING

Consider options

GET READY TO WATCH

Matt and Eva are looking over a chart that shows Traven Global's future coffee sales. Why do you think they look happy?

WATCH

(A) ■◀ **Watch the video. Was your guess correct?**

(B) ■◀ **Watch the video again. Answer the questions.**

1. Eva and Matt look at two charts. What do the charts show?

2. Why does Eva think the company needs to buy more coffee beans?

3. What does Eva suggest they do to increase warehouse space?

4. What does Matt think he can do in the warehouse?

CONVERSATION

(A) ■◀ **Watch part of the video.**
Complete the conversation.

Matt: We still don't have enough room in the

warehouse to _____ them all.

Eva: Well, the obvious solution is to just rent more space somewhere.

Matt: Well, that's one of our _____.
Gary said he would look into the cost of doing that. But I have a feeling it might be expensive.

Eva: And there's no way you can fit more product into the warehouse somehow?

Matt: Actually, that is another possibility. We could move some _____ around. We could also redo the shelving to stack everything higher.

Eva: So would that give us enough extra space?

Matt: Maybe.

(B) **PAIRS Practice the conversation.**

(C) **Read the conversation again. Underline two different options that Eva and Matt discuss for storing the coffee inventory.**

(D) **PAIRS Think of problems you have at work, school, or home. Then have your own conversations about the problems and different options to solve them.**

> **Pronunciation Note**
>
> Groups of consonant sounds can occur at the beginning, at the end, or in the middle of words.
>
> ◀))) **Listen and repeat. Notice that the letter _x_ is pronounced /ks/ in words with _x_ + consonant.**
>
> the next quarter   extra space
> The obvious solution is to rent more space.

> **Note**
>
> DISCUSS OPTIONS
> When you talk about how to solve a problem, you should discuss different options that you have. Consider the pros and cons of each option before you make any decisions.

WHAT DO YOU THINK?

GROUPS In the video, Matt says he isn't sure about the answer to Eva's question. Was he right to tell her that? Why do you think some people feel they have to give an answer, even if they aren't sure that it is correct?

Reported speech with modals

STUDY Reported Speech with Modals

Direct Speech	Reported Speech
She said, "You **must** pay the fine."	She said I **had to** pay the fine.
He said, "We **have to** arrive early."	He said we **had to** arrive early.
He told me, "I **will** call you tomorrow."	He told me he **would** call me the next day.
She told us, "I **can** pick it up."	She told us she **could** pick it up.

Grammar Note

The following modals do not change in reported speech: *should*, *could*, *would*, *ought to*, and *might*.

See page 155 for more information on this topic.

PRACTICE

A **Complete the sentences. Change direct speech to reported speech.**

1. Matt said, "We can solve the problem."

   Matt said _____they could_____ solve the problem.

2. The manager told us, "We might buy more inventory."

   The manager told us _____ buy more inventory.

3. Eva said, "I won't be able to leave until seven o'clock."

   Eva said _____ be able to leave until seven o'clock.

4. Gary told Kelly, "I have to attend a conference in Seattle next week."

   Gary told Kelly _____ to attend a conference in Seattle the following week.

5. The assistant said, "You should call to schedule an appointment with him."

   The assistant said _____ call to schedule an appointment with him.

B **Change the direct speech to reported speech. Use a separate piece of paper.**

1. Our teacher said, "You will pass the test if you study hard."

   > Our teacher said we would pass the test if we studied hard.

2. Jenny's supervisor told her, "I can let you have tomorrow off."

3. Tom said, "We should remember to buy Tina a birthday card."

4. The police officer said, "You must come to a complete stop at stop signs."

5. My friend told me, "We have to buy chips for the party."

WHAT ABOUT YOU?

GROUPS OF 3 **Student A:** Tell Student B something you must, will, can, should, or won't do.
Student B: Report A's statement to Student C. Then switch roles.

Chan: I have to go to the supermarket   *Lydia:* Chan said he had to go to the supermarket.

Identify supporting details

GET READY

Matt is reading a magazine article about places where people socialize and relax. Where do you go to socialize and relax?

READ

◀)) **Listen and read the article. Where do more and more people these days choose to socialize and relax?**

www.SocTrends.com

| Home | Web Trends | Viral Trends | Social Networking | Mobile Web | About Us |

The Third Place . . . Online?

People spend most of their time in two places: at work and at home. But many also have a "third place" where they socialize and relax. According to Ray Oldenburg, an urban sociologist, "third places" like coffee shops and parks are very important. Without a "third place" to go to, people can feel bored and lonely. Oldenburg worried that people are not gathering in these places as much as they used to do. But more and more people these days are getting together online. Can "third places" be found online? If so, is this a good or bad thing for our society?

To answer these questions, let's start by taking a closer look at the concept of "third place." A "third place" should be a warm and welcoming community, easily accessible, inexpensive, and open to all. Many people argue that chat rooms, virtual worlds, and social networking sites are all of these things. According to one stay-at-home mom, "My biggest social outlet is Twitter. The energy, kindness, ideas, and humor that are shared are off the charts some days."

In fact, online "third places" offer some advantages over real-world gathering places. For example, online, you can talk to people anywhere in the world, whenever you feel like it. You can also be someone you can't be in real life, especially in gaming virtual worlds. A shy person can be a leader, or an unattractive person can be beautiful. In addition, some people can't leave their houses due to physical disabilities or other problems. The Internet allows them to have a social life.

There are also, however, some disadvantages associated with online "third places." Because people do not always present themselves as they really are online, it's risky to share personal information with them. Also, when you are online, you are usually alone, staring at a screen. Most people prefer listening to, touching, and actually "doing things with" other people. Socializing online can also actually prevent people from interacting with others in the real world. We've all seen people who text instead of talking to others at parties. There is a concern that young people who spend a lot of time online may never learn to communicate effectively in the real world.

It seems clear that the "third place" is moving online for many of us. It's not as clear if this is a good or bad thing. Perhaps the answer is to spend time in "third places" in all the places that are available to us . . . in the real world and online.

AFTER YOU READ

A **Read the Reading Skill. Read the article again. Find the paragraph in which the main idea is that online "third places" have advantages over real-world "third places." Underline three details that support this main idea.**

B **Read the Reading Skill and the article again. Find the paragraph about the *dis*advantages associated with online "third places." Which of the following sentences are additional details that support the main idea of this paragraph? Check [✓] them.**

☐ Virtual worlds can be more satisfying than the real world.

☐ Some people spend all their free time on the Internet instead of developing rewarding relationships with people in the real world.

☐ Spending time online exposes you to the threat of identity theft.

☐ Children can learn valuable skills when they spend a lot of time online.

> ### Reading Skill
>
> **Supporting details** are facts, explanations, descriptions, or examples that are used to support an idea or opinion. In an article, supporting details give more information about the main idea or ideas, and they help you understand these ideas.

VOCABULARY STUDY Prefixes

> ### Build Your Vocabulary
>
> A **prefix** is a group of letters that you add to the beginning of a word in order to make a new word. Studying prefixes can help you understand the meaning of words. For example, the prefix *mis-* (= wrong) + *understand* = the new word *misunderstand*.

Read the Build Your Vocabulary note. Read the chart. What do the prefixes mean? Then complete the sentences with the words from the "Examples" column.

Prefix	Examples	Meaning
dis-	disabilities, disadvantage	
in-	inexpensive	
un-	unattractive	

1. I didn't have much money, so I bought the most _____ computer in the store.

2. Maria thought she was _____, so she didn't like to look in the mirror.

3. People with _____ cannot do some things that able-bodied people can do.

4. One _____ of trying to find a romantic partner online is that you don't know what the person really looks like until you meet him/her.

WHAT DO YOU THINK?

GROUPS Discuss: Is the fact that "third places" are moving online a good or bad thing for society? Support your opinion with details from the article or your own experience.

> **ON THE WEB**
>
> For more information, go online and search for an online "third place" that matches your own interests. Report back to the class what people do on the site and why it interests you.

7 Write about a problem and solutions

GET READY

Matt is reading an online article about dealing with annoying coworkers.
Have you ever had problems with annoying coworkers?

STUDY THE MODEL

A **Read the online article. How many different tips does the writer suggest
to help people solve the problem of annoying coworkers?**

www.SocTrends.com

CAREER: Annoying coworkers
Article #: 263291

Category: Career

We all need to get along with our coworkers. Sometimes that can be difficult because people often don't realize
that their behavior annoys others in the workplace. So it's important to deal effectively, but respectfully with the
problems that annoying coworkers cause. Here are a few tips on how to do that.

One way to deal with annoying coworkers is to speak directly to them about a problem. At my last job, I sat next to
a woman named "Anna" (not her real name). She was loud, especially on the phone. This made it difficult for me to
concentrate on my work. So one day I said to her, "I'm sorry, but it's hard to concentrate when you're on the phone.
Do you think you could talk a little more quietly?" Anna immediately apologized. She hadn't realized she had been
speaking so loudly. Being direct solved the problem right away.

Sometimes you want a coworker's behavior to change, but you don't feel comfortable being so direct. I had a
coworker named "Jim" who often interrupted me at work. He would sit down in my cubicle and talk about his
personal life. Again, I couldn't get my work done. I didn't want to hurt his feelings, so I didn't tell him to leave.
I gave him a hint instead. Jim liked to sit in a comfortable chair facing my desk. I moved the chair to the other side
of the cubicle and put a pile of books on it. I never said anything to Jim directly. Moving the chair was enough,
and he stopped visiting me.

In some cases the best solution is to discuss the problem with your manager. "Liz" was a very nice person,
but she liked to spray her cubicle with a strong-smelling air freshener. I have allergies, and I could smell it from
my cubicle. I knew that other people were unhappy about the smell, too. So, a group of us talked to the manager.
He made a new rule: Employees were not allowed to use air freshener sprays in the office. Everyone was relieved,
and because the message came from the manager, Liz never realized that we had complained about her.

So if one of your coworkers becomes annoying, you can try speaking directly to him/her, giving an indirect hint,
or talking to your manager about the problem. I hope these tips will help you with your own coworkers!

Find Jobs | Job Recommendations | Post Résumés | Advice & Resources

B **Read the Writing Tip. Then look at the Model again.
Underline the thesis statement in the first paragraph.**

C **Read the Writing Tip and the Model again.
Does the thesis statement tell the solution(s)?
If not, which sentences in the essay do? Circle them.**

Writing Tip

The **thesis statement** is one or
more sentences that present the
main idea of a piece of writing. In
a **problem-and-solution** essay, the
thesis statement tells the problem.
It may also tell the solution, or the
solution may be discussed later, in
the body and conclusion.

D Look at the T-chart the writer used and complete it with information from the Model.

Problem: _____ and the problems they cause	**Solution 1:** Speak _____ _____.
	Solution 2: Give _____ _____.
	Solution 3: Talk to your _____ _____.

BEFORE YOU WRITE

A **PAIRS** Think about common problems that people have in the workplace. Then make a list of possible solutions to the problems.

B You're going to write a few paragraphs about one of the workplace problems you discussed in Exercise A. Suggest three solutions to the problem. Use the T-chart below to plan your paragraphs.

Problem: _____ _____	**Solution 1:** _____ _____ _____
	Solution 2: _____ _____ _____
	Solution 3: _____ _____ _____

WRITE

Write about a workplace problem and suggest solutions to the problem.
Review the Model and the Writing Tip. Use the ideas in your T-chart.
Use a separate piece of paper.

LISTENING AND SPEAKING

8 Make a decision

GET READY TO WATCH

Matt and Gary are making an important decision. When was the last time you had to make an important decision?

WATCH

◀ **Watch the video. Answer the questions.**

1. What have Gary, Eva, and Matt already agreed to do?

2. What would be more expensive: renting more warehouse space or reorganizing the warehouse?

3. How long would it take to reorganize the warehouse?

4. What do Gary and Matt decide to do?

CONVERSATION

A ◀ **Watch part of the video. Complete the conversation.**

Matt: We should consider reorganizing the warehouse instead of renting more space. Greg and I figured out how much it would cost.

Look, we _____ this business plan.

Gary: OK . . . So walk me through this. How much *would* it cost?

Matt: Well, we'd have to pay for new shelving materials and equipment.

I've _____ the costs in this column.

Gary: Hmm. You're right. It would definitely be cheaper than renting more space. . . . And how long would it take you and your staff to make these changes?

Matt: A few weeks.

Gary: OK . . . yeah, that seems doable.

Matt: If we reorganize, we'll benefit in the long run because the warehouse will

become more _____. So, I really think this is a better solution than renting more space.

Gary: I agree. . . . OK, that settles it for me. Let's buy the Brazilian beans— and reorganize the warehouse.

B PAIRS **Practice the conversation.**

C **Read the conversation again. Underline the final decision(s).**

D PAIRS **Have similar conversations. Discuss different options and then come to a final decision about how to solve a problem.**

WHAT DO YOU THINK?

GROUPS In the video, what do Gary and Matt do to make sure that they make the best possible decision? Do you think that reorganizing the warehouse is the best choice for them? Explain your answer.

Sal Morales   *Today*
I've always been an accountant, but maybe some other job would suit me better . . . ?

GET READY

Sal is going to research different kinds of occupations.
What kind of information do you think he should try to find out?

RESEARCH JOBS

A **Read Sal's chart. Answer the questions.**

	Financial Advisor	Loan Officer	Accountant
Location	Finance, insurance companies; many are self-employed	Banks, mortgage companies	Many different companies
Working hours	Irregular; many nights and weekends	Full-time; often work longer hours	Usually 40 hours per week
Median pay	$64,750/year	$56,490/year	$61,690/year
Job description	Meet with clients to help them with investments, taxes, and insurance decisions; create financial plans	Evaluate, authorize, or recommend approval of loan applications	Prepare and check financial records; ensure that taxes are paid; help organizations run efficiently
Skills	Math, problem-solving, computer, and analytical skills; interpersonal and sales skills	Math and communication skills	Math, computer, and communication skills; attention to detail; analytical
Entry-level education required	Bachelor's degree; master's degree helpful	High school diploma	Bachelor's degree in accounting
Job outlook, 2010–20	32% growth	14% growth	16% growth

Source: Bureau of Labor Statistics Occupational Outlook Handbook

1. Which occupation has the highest salary?
2. Which has the most complex job duties and requires the most skills?
3. Which requires the most education?
4. Which has the best job outlook for the future?

B **PAIRS** **After doing this research, Sal decided to apply for accountant positions. Why do you think he decided to do that?**

PUT YOUR IDEAS TO WORK

ON THE WEB

Research the jobs that interest you online. Check the information in your chart and add more.

A **Make a list of 3 different kinds of occupations that you want to find out more about. Choose jobs that match your skills and interests.**

B See page 158 for a job research chart. **Complete the chart with everything you know about the occupations. Use Sal's chart as a model.**

GRAMMAR
See page 146 for your Grammar Review.

VOCABULARY See page 161 for the Unit 2 Vocabulary.

Vocabulary Learning Strategy: Learn Words That Go Together

A Find words from the list that are used together. Fill in the missing words.

make _____ _____   stuck _____   _____ event

_____ control   _____ emissions   retail _____

_____ _____ the pace   stock _____ _____   social _____ _____

in _____ _____ run   put _____   entry- _____

B Circle 5 groups of words in Exercise A that are used together.
Write a sentence with each one.

SPELLING See page 161 for the Unit 2 Vocabulary.

CLASS Choose 10 words or phrases for a spelling test.

LISTENING PLUS

Watch each video. Write the story of Matt's day on a separate piece of paper.

> Matt was planning to go fishing, but Gary called him to his office. Gary wants
> to talk to Matt about buying Brazilian coffee beans. . . .

NOW I CAN

PAIRS **See page 19 for the Unit 2 Goals.** Check ☑ the things you can do.
Underline the things you want to study more. Then share your information
with a partner.

I can _____. I need more practice with _____.

3 Gary Helps Out

MY GOALS

☐ Check on progress

☐ Compare an invoice and a purchase order

☐ Ask for advice

☐ Identify needs

☐ Set goals

Go to MyEnglishLab for more practice after each lesson.

Gary Frye

Gary   *Today*
Some people on my staff are struggling today. I'm doing my best to help them out.

LISTENING AND SPEAKING

Check on progress

GET READY TO WATCH

Matt is using a new kind of computer software.
How do you think he feels about it?

WATCH

A ▶️ **Watch the video. Was your guess correct?**

B ▶️ **Watch the video again. Answer the questions.**

1. Why are some of the workers having trouble with the new system?

2. What two kinds of support did the software company provide?

3. What kind of training does Matt suggest?

4. What happens when Matt tries to show Gary how the ordering system works?

CONVERSATION

A ▶️ **Watch part of the video.
Complete the conversation.**

Gary: So how's it going with the new _____?

Matt: Well, it took me a while to figure out how to use it.
But I think I've got the hang of it now.

Gary: OK, good. What about the online ordering

_____? It's working out pretty well, isn't it?

Matt: For the most part, yes, it is. But some of the guys
in the warehouse are having trouble getting used to it.

Gary: Why, exactly?

Matt: The screen is a little difficult to use. It's easy to make a _____. Take a look.

Pronunciation Note

In tag questions, the voice goes up
on the tag if we are asking a question
to check or confirm information.

🔊 **Listen and repeat.**

They've completed the online training,
haven't they?

B PAIRS **Practice the conversation.**

C **Read the conversation again. Underline questions Gary asks to check on progress.**

D PAIRS **Think of a task you are working on now at home, school, or work.
Describe the task to your partner. Then have your own conversations. Check on the
progress of your partner's task, and ask and answer questions about it.**

WHAT DO YOU THINK?

GROUPS In the video, Gary checks on Matt's progress. Why is it important to check on
employees' progress in work situations?

GRAMMAR

Tag questions

STUDY Tag Questions

Affirmative Statement	Negative Tag
They finished the project,	**didn't they?**
You're from Peru,	**aren't you?**
She has seen the invoice,	**hasn't she?**
He should apply for the job,	**shouldn't he?**

Negative Statement	Affirmative Tag
You won't forget to call me,	**will you?**
He can't help us,	**can he?**
She doesn't have to go,	**does she?**

Grammar Note

- Use tag questions to confirm or check information.
- For most verbs, use *do* as an auxiliary verb in the tag.

PRACTICE

A **Circle the correct words.**

1. They attended the meeting, **didn't** / **did** they?

2. You'll call me if there's a problem, **won't** / **will** you?

3. Martin doesn't like the new ordering system, **does** / **doesn't** he?

4. That online training wasn't very useful, **did** / **was** it?

5. You've learned how to use the new software, **didn't** / **haven't** you?

6. She can't operate a forklift, **can't** / **can** she?

B **Complete the tag questions.**

1. You received my email yesterday, ___didn't you___?

2. John can't use a computer very well, _____?

3. She doesn't need more training, _____?

4. You have to work this weekend, _____?

5. Her name is Young Sun, _____?

6. He's worked here for five years, _____?

WHAT ABOUT YOU?

GROUPS Write down 4 things you think you know about the people in your class. Then ask tag questions to confirm the information.

Paolo is from Brazil, isn't he?

Bo speaks Cantonese, doesn't he?

PRACTICAL SKILLS

Compare an invoice and a purchase order

 GET READY

Gary Frye sometimes needs to sign off on purchase orders and invoices.
Have you ever filled out or received purchase orders or invoices?

PRACTICAL READING

A **Read the purchase order and the invoice on page 37. Which document did Traven Global create and send to another company in order to buy products?**

B **Read the purchase order and invoice again. Circle the correct words.**

1. We received a purchase order / an invoice from the furniture store for the desks we ordered, so we should pay it soon.

2. The unit price / quantity of this pen is $5.

3. Every company assigns an item number / a cartridge to each product so that it can identify it.

4. The product's name is in the quantity / description column of the invoice.

5. Add the tax to the total / subtotal to figure out how much they have to pay.

6. Our state charges sales tax / quantity on the products sold in its stores.

C **Read the documents again. Answer the questions.**

1. What is the quantity of computers on the purchase order?
   What is the quantity of computers on the invoice?

2. What is the computer price listed on the purchase order? The invoice?

3. Which type of printer is listed on the purchase order? The invoice?

4. What is the printer price listed on the purchase order? The invoice?

5. What kind of printer cartridge is listed on the purchase order? The invoice?

6. What is the total listed on the purchase order? The invoice?

PRACTICAL LISTENING

🔊)) **Listen to the podcast about purchase orders and invoices. Answer the questions.**

1. When does a company create a purchase order?

2. When does a company send an invoice?

3. What happens when a purchase order and an invoice don't match?

4. What are the most common mistakes in purchase orders and invoices?

5. What should you do if you have questions about a purchase order or invoice?

WHAT DO YOU THINK?

GROUPS Review the purchase order, invoice, and podcast. What mistakes do you see
in the purchase order and invoice? What should Gary do about the mistakes?

Purchase Order

Traven Global Coffee

Date: 08-10-14
P.O.#: 34578
Customer ID: CT432

Vendor: Computer Tree
785 Coral View Dr.
Miami, FL 33127

Ship to: Traven Global Coffee
3818 N. Miami Ave.
Miami, FL 33127

Shipping Method: Go Pack Courier

Delivery Date: 08-15-14

Quantity	Item No.	Description	Job	Unit Price	Amount
10	C987	Computer	2341	$399.00	$3,990.00
1	P231	Printer, four color	2341	$299.00	$ 299.00
1	PC841	Printer cartridge	2341	$89.99	$ 89.99
				Subtotal	$4,378.99
				Tax	$ 218.95
				Total	**$4,597.94**

INVOICE

Computer Tree
785 Coral View Drive
Miami, FL 33127

Sold to: Traven Global Coffee
3818 N. Miami Ave.
Miami, FL 33127

Invoice No.	
Invoice Date	
Our Order No.	34578
Your Order No.	
Terms	
Sales Rep	Abby Wooly
Shipped Via	
Prepaid or collect	

Quantity	Description	Unit Price	Amount
12	C987: Computer	$399.00	$4,788.00
1	P238: Printer, four color	$349.00	$ 349.00
1	PC841: Printer cartridge	$89.99	$ 89.99
		Subtotal	$5,226.99
		Tax	$ 261.35
		Total	**$5,488.34**

4 Ask for advice

GET READY TO WATCH

Eva is worried about her MBA classes.
Why do you think she is worried?

WATCH

A ◼◀ **Watch the video. Was your guess correct?**

B ◼◀ **Watch the video again. Answer the questions.**

1. What is Eva considering doing?

2. What are Eva's responsibilities?

3. What does Gary tell her to do?

4. How is Gary going to try to help Eva?

CONVERSATION

A ◼◀ **Watch part of the video.
Complete the conversation.**

Eva: Gary, could I ask your _____
about something?

Gary: Sure! What's going on?

Eva: I'm considering _____ of the
program. Last quarter, I had to drop one of
my classes.

Gary: You did? What happened?

Eva: Well, I've been working, caring for two kids, *and* taking two classes.
Before last quarter, I had never tried to do all those things at the
same time. I guess it was just too much for me.

Gary: I see. It *is* hard to balance all those _____.

Eva: So what do you think I should do?

Gary: Well, if I were you, I would stay in school.

B PAIRS **Practice the conversation.**

C **Read the conversation again. Underline Gary's advice.**

D PAIRS **Have your own conversations. Switch roles.**
Student A: Ask your partner for advice on a problem you are having.
Student B: Offer advice.

> **Pronunciation Note**
>
> To show interest or surprise, we can ask
> a short question, making the voice go up
> high at the end.
>
> ◀⟩⟩ **Listen and repeat the questions.**
>
> (I had to drop one of my classes.)
> You **did**?↗
>
> (If I were you, I would stay in school.)
> You **would**?↗

WHAT DO YOU THINK?

GROUPS What are the pros and cons of raising a family, working, and going to school all at
the same time? Do you agree with the advice Gary gives Eva in the video?

Past perfect and past perfect continuous

STUDY Past Perfect and Past Perfect Continuous

Past Perfect

Subject	*had*	Past Participle	
They	had	delivered	the order by the time he called.

Past Perfect Continuous

	Subject	*had been*	Present Participle	
By 2012,	Ana	had been	taking	classes for years.

Grammar Note

· Use the past perfect to talk about something that happened before a certain time in the past.
· Use the past perfect continuous to talk about something that continued for a while or was in progress before a certain time in the past.

See page 156 for more information on this topic.

PRACTICE

A Circle the correct forms. Use the past perfect continuous form when possible.

1. By the time the sun went down, she had **read** / **been reading** for hours.

2. When classes started, she had still not **bought** / **been buying** her textbooks.

3. The company had already **tried** / **been trying** to help employees get college degrees for years when they introduced the scholarship program.

4. I had just **finished** / **been finishing** my homework when you walked in.

5. By 2013, Pedro had **completed** / **been completing** his master's degree.

B Complete the sentences. Use the past perfect or past perfect continuous form of the verbs. Use the past perfect continuous form when possible.

1. Before Jin turned 15, he ___*had moved*___ to the United States.
   _{move}

2. Linda _____ at the hospital for ten years when she was finally promoted.
   _{work}

3. By the time she took the GED test, Solange _____ English for six years.
   _{study}

4. Perry _____ a salesman for six months when he decided to find a new job.
   _{be}

5. By 2005, Ivana _____ her first child.
   _{have}

WHAT ABOUT YOU?

PAIRS Talk about 2 things you had done by an important date in your past. Then talk about 2 things you had been doing by an important date.

Before I finished high school, I had made the decision to leave my country.

By the time I bought my apartment, I had been living in Los Angeles for 10 years.

Make connections between related information

GET READY

Gary is reading an article on stress management. Do you sometimes feel stressed out? What do you do to relieve stress?

READ

◀))) **Listen and read the article. What does the author think everyone should spend more time doing?**

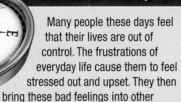

REFLECT, REST, RESET

Many people these days feel that their lives are out of control. The frustrations of everyday life cause them to feel stressed out and upset. They then bring these bad feelings into other situations in their lives in a process that psychologists call "negative spill." How can people manage their stress? Dr. Adam Fraser, the author of *The Third Space: Using Life's Little Transitions to Find Balance and Happiness*, may have the answer.

Like many other psychologists, Dr. Fraser feels that people are stressed out because they don't spend enough time relaxing and thinking. But many people feel that they simply don't have time to relax. According to Fraser, we all have time to relax, as long as we think in terms of short breaks rather than hours. Fraser thinks we should use time that we are currently "wasting"—the transitional time between the different activities in our day—to relax and think. He calls this transitional time the "Third Space."

Let's look at a specific example. Suppose you're on your way to an important job interview. You turn the ignition key, but your car won't start. The battery is dead. You jump the battery and drive to the job interview. Will you

burst into tears or arrive at the interview angry and upset, still reliving the stress of dealing with the dead battery? Or will you be calm and in control? It all depends on what you think and feel in the "Third Space" in this situation— the time you spend driving on your way to the interview.

Fraser recommends that we use transitional time to do three things: reflect, rest, and reset. What do these terms mean?

- **Reflect.** Think about the experience you just had. Focus on what you achieved, not what you failed to do. This can put a stressful experience in a more positive light.

- **Rest.** Do something that relaxes you, such as reading or exercising. This will help you get your mind off of your problems.

- **Reset.** Think about how you want to act during the next activity on your schedule. Visualize your success. This will make it more likely that you will succeed.

So the next time you have a stressful experience, try Dr. Fraser's techniques. Make an effort to reflect, rest, and reset during your transition time to the next activity in your day. You may find yourself feeling calmer, happier, and more successful.

According to the Bureau of Labor Statistics, in 2010, Americans only took 17 minutes a day to relax and think. Perhaps we should consider increasing that time?

Leisure time (in minutes) on an average day:

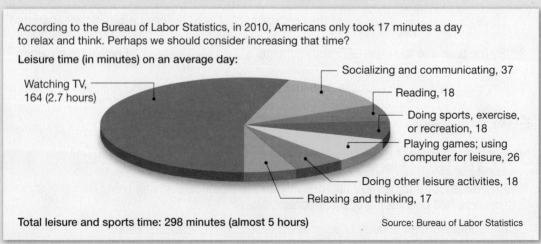

Watching TV, 164 (2.7 hours)

Socializing and communicating, 37

Reading, 18

Doing sports, exercise, or recreation, 18

Playing games; using computer for leisure, 26

Doing other leisure activities, 18

Relaxing and thinking, 17

Total leisure and sports time: 298 minutes (almost 5 hours)

Source: Bureau of Labor Statistics

AFTER YOU READ

A Read the Reading Skill. Read the article again. Look at the pie chart. Underline the sentence in the article that is most closely related to the information in the pie chart.

B Look at the pie chart again. Answer the questions.

1. How much time does the average American spend doing sports and leisure activities every day?

2. Does the average American spend more time reading or socializing?

3. Does the average American spend more time exercising or thinking?

4. Which activity does the average American spend the most leisure time doing?

Reading Skill

To understand an article, readers sometimes need to **make connections between related information** in different sections of the article. For example, an illustration or chart may give information that supports a sentence or paragraph in an article. A certain topic might also appear in different sections of an article, such as in the introduction and the conclusion.

VOCABULARY STUDY Collocations

Build Your Vocabulary

Collocations are groups of words that are often used together. People remember them as wholes. The words used together can be of different types, such as adjective + noun, verb + prepositional phrase, or verb + noun. For example: *do the dishes; a big mistake.* Learning collocations can help make your English sound more natural.

Read the Build Your Vocabulary note. Then read the collocations in the word box. Find and underline them in the article. (They may be in a different form.) Then complete the paragraph with some of the collocations. Use the correct form.

be in control	be out of control	burst into tears
dead battery	feel stressed out	get his mind off of
leisure activity	make an effort	spend time

Eric's life (1) _____ right now—he has too much to do, and he

(2) _____ all the time. He needs to (3) _____ to relax more,

or he'll never be happy. He should (4) _____ his problems by taking a yoga

class. He could also (5) _____ with his friends because that seems to relax

him. If he does all these things, I'm sure his life will (6) _____ again soon.

WHAT DO YOU THINK?

GROUPS Do you think Dr. Fraser's advice can help people reduce their stress? Do you plan to try any of these strategies yourself? Explain why or why not.

ON THE WEB

For more information, go online and search "reducing stress." Find a new tip for reducing stress and report back to the class.

7 Write a business letter

GET READY

Gary is writing a letter to a local elected official to make a request.
Have you ever written to an elected official? What did you write about?

STUDY THE MODEL

A **Read the letter. What is Gary asking for?**

Gary Frye
9427 SW 114th St.
Miami, FL 33176
(305) 555-9821
garyfrye@gimail.com

Commissioner Sally Torres
District 8   March 30, 2014
Stephen P. Clark Center
111 NW 1st Street, Suite 220
Miami, Florida 33128

Dear Commissioner Torres,

I live in Kendall, close to the intersection of the Killian Parkway and SW 96th
Avenue. I'm writing to request that the city add traffic lights at this intersection.

As you know, Killian Parkway can get very busy. Traffic is heavy during rush hour.
Sometimes I have to wait for several minutes before I can make the turn onto the
parkway in the morning. If there were traffic lights, vehicles would take turns
crossing the intersection, and traffic would move more quickly.

When it isn't rush hour, on the other hand, cars drive much too fast down Killian
Parkway. Both drivers and pedestrians are at risk. Three weeks ago, I witnessed an
accident at Killian Parkway and SW 96th Avenue. A taxi and a pickup truck crashed
into each other. Luckily, no one was seriously hurt. Yesterday, I was nearly involved
in an accident myself. I was walking across Killian Parkway, and a car nearly hit me.
I would also like to point out many children walk around in the neighborhood; there
are several schools and a large park nearby. Traffic lights would force speeding cars
to slow down. This would improve safety for both drivers and pedestrians.

The traffic lights I'm proposing would improve our neighborhood in two
important ways. They would help traffic move more quickly during rush hour, and
they would prevent accidents. I hope you will make the decision to add traffic lights
at the intersection of Killian Parkway and SW 96th Avenue soon.

Sincerely yours,

Gary Frye

Gary Frye, Concerned Citizen

B Read the Writing Tip. Read the Model again. Circle and label each part of Gary's letter with the business letter sections listed in the Writing Tip.

C Look at the business letter template the writer used and complete it with information from the Model.

Sender's contact information

Name: _Gary Frye_

Address: _____

City, State, Zip Code: _____

Phone Number: _(305) 555-9821_

Email Address: _garyfrye@gimail.com_

Date: _____

Recipient's contact information

Name/Title: _____

Address 1: _Stephen P. Clark Center_

Address 2: _____

City, State, Zip Code: _Miami, FL 33128_

Dear _____,

Introduction: _writing to request_ _____ _at_ _____ .

Body Paragraph 1: _Killian Parkway has heavy_ _____ _during_

_____ . _____ _would make traffic move more_

_____ .

Body Paragraph 2: _Cars speed on Killian Parkway. There are_ _____

_____ . _____ _would force cars to_

down. _____

Conclusion: _____ _would improve neighborhood in_

important ways. I hope you will make the decision

to add them soon.

BEFORE YOU WRITE

A PAIRS Make a list of things you want to change in your community.

B You're going to write a letter to an elected official, asking him/her to make one of the changes you discussed in Exercise A. Use a business letter template to plan your letter. Use a separate piece of paper.

WRITE

Write a business letter to an official. Review the Model and the Writing Tip. Use the ideas in your business letter template. Use a separate piece of paper.

Writing Tip

When writing a formal letter, it's a good idea to use **business letter format**. Keep your letter simple, focused, and polite. Include the following sections:

· Sender's contact information
· Date
· Recipient's contact information
· Greeting
· Introduction (introduce topic of letter)
· Body paragraphs (give more details about topic)
· Conclusion (restate topic)
· Salutation

GET READY TO WATCH

Gary and Kelly Chen are talking about in-house training. Have you ever attended a training session at your workplace? What did you learn?

WATCH

■◀ **Watch the video. Answer the questions.**

1. What does Gary ask Kelly to do?

2. Why does Kelly ask Gary questions and take notes on his answers?

3. What are the warehouse workers having problems with?

4. What do Kelly and Gary say about Matt at the end of the video?

CONVERSATION

A ■◀ **Watch part of the video. Complete the conversation.**

Kelly: Let me just make sure we're on the same _____ about what the guys need. I have a couple of questions.

Gary: OK, shoot.

Kelly: First of all, can you give me an idea of what exactly they're having trouble with?

Gary: They're having problems with _____ the customer orders. Someone needs to show them how to do it in a step-by-step way.

Kelly: OK, processing the customer orders. We can work on that. Is that it?

Gary: Sometimes the invoices are wrong, too. Those need to be _____ before they're processed.

Kelly: All right. We can go over how to handle the invoices. Anything else?

Gary: Not that I'm aware of.

B PAIRS **Practice the conversation.**

C **Read the conversation again. Underline the places where Kelly identifies Gary's needs.**

D PAIRS **Have your own conversations.**
Student A: Talk about something you need at home, school, or work.
Student B: Ask questions to find out more about what your partner needs.

WHAT DO YOU THINK?

GROUPS In the video, Gary and Kelly think that hands-on training is the best way to learn how to use the new software. Can you think of other skills that are best learned by doing the action yourself?

Sal Morales *Today*
My task for today: figuring out my long-term and short-term career goals.

GET READY

Sal needs to set career goals for himself. Have you ever set goals for yourself? Which goals did you set, and did you achieve them?

SET GOALS

Read Sal's long-term and short-term career goals. Answer the questions.

Long-Term Career Goals	Time Frame
1. To find an accountant position	within three months
2. To be promoted to Accounting Manager	within five years
3. To be promoted to Chief Financial Officer	within 20 years
4. To retire	within 30 years

Short-Term/Enabling Goals	
These goals will enable me to: find an accountant position	
Goal	Dates
1. Check employment ads online, in newspapers	February 15–April 15
2. Network with friends, contacts online, etc.	February 15–April 15
3. Update résumé and cover letter	February 15–18
4. Send out job applications	February 18–May 1
5. Arrange interviews with companies	February 21–May 15
6. Prepare for interviews (research companies, etc.)	February 23–May 15
7. Go on interviews	February 25–May 15
8. Follow up on interviews with thank-you letters	February 26–May 30

1. Which long-term goal does Sal want to achieve first?

2. What is Sal's final long-term career goal before he retires?

3. What will Sal's list of short-term goals enable him to do?

4. What short-term goal does he plan to achieve after he updates his résumé?

5. What is Sal's final short-term goal?

PUT YOUR IDEAS TO WORK

A Using Sal's goals as a model, make a chart of your long-term career goals. Include time frames. Use a separate piece of paper.

B Make a list of short-term goals that will enable you to achieve one of your long-term goals. What do you need to do in the next days, weeks, or months to make progress towards the goal?

C PAIRS Can you suggest any other short-term goals that might enable your partner to make progress towards his/her long-term goal?

GRAMMAR
See page 147 for your Grammar Review.

VOCABULARY See page 161 for the Unit 3 Vocabulary.

Vocabulary Learning Strategy: Use Familiar Words or Images to Remember Phrases

A Find compound words or phrases from the list that contain familiar words that you can easily visualize or draw pictures of. Fill in the blanks.

_____hands-on_____   _____

_____   _____

B Write a sentence with each word or phrase from Exercise A.

SPELLING See page 161 for the Unit 3 Vocabulary.

CLASS Choose 10 words for a spelling test.

LISTENING PLUS

Watch each video. Write the story of Gary's day on a separate piece of paper.

> *Gary drops by Matt's office. He wants to check on Matt's progress with the new software. Matt is having some trouble with it. . . .*

NOW I CAN

PAIRS See page 33 for the Unit 3 Goals. Check ☑ the things you can do. Underline the things you want to study more. Then share your information with a partner.

> I can _____. I need more practice with _____.

4

Kelly, the People Person

MY GOALS

☐ Ask for help

☐ Interpret a rental agreement

☐ Talk about interests and skills

☐ Give instructions

☐ Interpret employment ads

Go to MyEnglishLab for more practice after each lesson.

Kelly Chen

Kelly   *Today*
The best thing about working in HR is helping people with their careers. I love that!

1 Ask for help

GET READY TO WATCH

Walt and Kelly are in Kelly's office. What do you think Walt is doing? What is Kelly doing?

WATCH

A ◼◀ **Watch the video. Were your guesses correct?**

B ◼◀ **Watch the video again. Answer the questions.**

1. Why did Walt come to Kelly's office?

2. What does Walt ask for help with?

3. What does Kelly say she will do?

CONVERSATION

A ◼◀ **Watch part of the video. Complete the conversation.**

Walt: Have you given the new _____ their assignments yet?

Kelly: No, not yet.

Walt: OK, good. Can I ask you to keep the marketing department in mind when you do that? We could really use some help.

Kelly: OK. Thanks for letting me know.

Walt: We need someone with good _____ skills. Ever since the new company website went live, we've been getting lots of comments from users.

It would be great if the intern could help us keep _____ of them all.

Kelly: I'll make a note of that.

Walt: Also, could you give us someone who knows something about marketing? I need help with my market research.

Kelly: Sure.

B PAIRS **Practice the conversation.**

C **Read the conversation again. Underline two places where Walt asks for help.**

D PAIRS **Have your own conversations. Ask your partner for help with something at home, school, or work.**

WHAT DO YOU THINK?

GROUPS In the video, Kelly says she will try to find out if the new intern can help Walt. What questions do you think she will ask the new intern?

2 Object + infinitive after certain verbs

STUDY Object + Infinitive After Certain Verbs

Subject	Verb	Object	Infinitive
She	**wants**	him	**to work** in her department.
I	**told**	him	**to come** in tomorrow.
He	**invited**	them	**to attend** the conference.
I	**have warned**	her	**to be** more careful.

See page 156 for a list of verbs followed by object + infinitive.

> **Grammar Note**
> · Use an object + an infinitive after verbs of permission or obligation, such as *allow* and *force*.
> · Form the negative by placing *not* between the object and infinitive: *I told him not to come in tomorrow.*

PRACTICE

A Complete the paragraph. Unscramble the words.

Ben is the mailroom manager at a small company. He
<u>asked the Human Resources manager to assign</u> an intern to the mailroom.
     1. asked / to assign / the Human Resources manager

He _____ him sort and deliver packages.
     2. the intern / wanted / to help

There was only one intern available, and several departments needed help. So the

HR manager _____ the Operations
     3. to contact / Ben / told

manager of the company and explain his situation. The Operations manager

_____ the new intern to the mailroom.
     4. authorized / to send / the HR manager

B Complete the list of workplace rules for interns. Use the correct forms of the words.

1. The company __<u>requires you to attend</u>__ an orientation session.
     require / you / attend

2. We _____ casually in the office.
     expect / you / not / dress

3. We _____ in the employee parking lot.
     permit / interns / park

4. If anyone _____ something you are not comfortable with,
     order / you / do

   we _____ HR immediately.
     encourage / you / contact

5. During the summer, the company _____ work at 1 P.M. every Friday.
     allow / employees / leave

WHAT ABOUT YOU?

PAIRS Talk about two things that someone expected or permitted you to do. Then talk about two things that you asked or told others to do.

My boss expected me to work overtime every day.   *I asked my daughter not to come home late.*

GET READY

Kelly wants to rent a new apartment. She is reviewing the rental or lease agreement for the apartment. Have you ever signed a rental agreement?

PRACTICAL READING

A **Scan the rental agreement. How many people want to rent the apartment?**

Residential Lease Agreement

THIS LEASE AGREEMENT is entered into this 1st day of March, 2014, by _Eddie Tocco_ , the "Landlord" and _Kelly and Paul Chen_ , the "Tenant."

1. The Landlord leases to the Tenant and the Tenant leases from the Landlord, upon the terms and conditions below, the dwelling located at _700 Ives Dairy Rd., Apt. 12, North Miami Beach, FL_ for the period starting on the 1st day of March, 2014, and ending on the 1st day of March, 2015. After the 1st of March, 2015, this Lease Agreement shall automatically renew each year unless terminated in writing. The Tenant is required to give the Landlord in writing a notice one month (30 days) in advance of his/her moving. Notice must be given on the first day of a month. If notice is given after the first day of the month, the one-month (30-day) notice will not start until the following month. Rent may be increased at any time after the first year.

2. The Tenant shall pay as rent the sum of $ 1,200.00 per month. Rent is due and payable monthly, in advance, no later than 5:00 P.M. by the fourth day of every month. Tenant further agrees to pay a late charge of $25.00 for each day rent is not received after the fourth of the month to the Landlord, regardless of the cause.

3. The dwelling shall be used and occupied solely by the Tenant and the Tenant's immediate family, consisting of _Kelly and Paul Chen_ , exclusively, as a private single family dwelling. No part of the dwelling shall be used at any time during the term of this Florida Lease Agreement by the Tenant for the purpose of carrying on any business, profession, or trade of any kind. It may not be used for any purpose other than as a private single family dwelling. The Tenant shall not allow any other person to use or occupy the dwelling without first obtaining the Landlord's written consent.

4. Tenant agrees to accept the property in its current condition and to return it in "moving-in clean" condition, or to pay a special cleaning charge of $200.00 upon vacating the premises.

5. THERE WILL BE NO ANIMALS. The Tenant shall not permit any animal, including mammals, reptiles, birds, fish, rodents, or insects on the property, even temporarily, unless otherwise agreed upon in a separate written Pet Agreement. If the Tenant violates the pet restrictions of this Lease, the Tenant will pay to the Landlord a fee of $10.00 per day per animal for each day.

B **Read the rental agreement again. Then complete the sentences. Use the words from the box.**

consent   in advance   notice   renew   restriction   vacate

1. I paid two months' rent _____ when I moved in.
2. Did you give the landlord a month's _____ before you moved out?
3. She plans to _____ the apartment soon, so we'll need a new tenant.
4. The Mendozas want to _____ their lease because they like the house.
5. There's a pet _____ in the lease, so we can't get a dog.
6. Did you get written _____ from the landlord before you painted the apartment?

C **Read the rental agreement again. Answer the questions.**

1. Who is the landlord?
2. Where is the apartment?
3. How many months is the lease?
4. When does the tenant have to tell the landlord he/she is moving out?
5. When can the landlord raise the rent?
6. How much is the rent?
7. What happens if the tenant does not pay the rent on time?
8. Who is allowed to live in the apartment?
9. What condition should the apartment be in when the tenant moves out?
10. What kinds of pets are allowed?

D **Kelly's husband Paul is a lawyer with his own practice, and he works from home. Kelly and Paul also have a cat. Underline the sections of the lease that might cause problems for them.**

PRACTICAL LISTENING

🔊)) **Listen to the podcast about rental agreements. Answer the questions.**

1. If you're a tenant, what should you bring with you when you meet a landlord?
2. If you have questions about the lease, who can you ask for help?
3. What are some changes you might be able to make to a lease?
4. Why should you walk through the property with the landlord?
5. When is the best time to ask for repairs?

WHAT DO YOU THINK?

GROUPS Kelly and Paul really like the apartment. Before they can rent the apartment, what changes can or should they ask the landlord to make to the lease?

4

Talk about interests and skills

GET READY TO WATCH

Kelly has an appointment with the new intern, Marie Sylvain. How do you feel when you meet someone for the first time in a workplace setting?

WATCH

■◄ **Watch the video. Answer the questions.**

1. How does Marie feel about coffee?
2. Why is Kelly happy that the interns will be working at the company?
3. What does Marie want to do after she graduates?
4. Who will give Marie more details about her job duties?

CONVERSATION

A ■◄ **Watch part of the video. Complete the conversation.**

Kelly: Can you tell me a little more about your interests and skills?

Marie: Well, I'm very interested in

_____.

Kelly: Oh, really?

Marie: Yes. I've taken a lot of marketing classes, and

I'm eager to get some _____ experience. My goal is to work in marketing after I graduate.

Kelly: I see.

Marie: And I'm very good with computers.

Kelly: Tell me more.

Marie: I'm _____ in a lot of different programs. I can design websites. I maintain the site for the student union at my college and . . .

Pronunciation Note

Some words have a vowel that is often dropped when we say the word in conversation.

◄)) **Listen and repeat.**

intérests	différent	sevéral
despérately	intérested	actuálly

B PAIRS **Practice the conversation.**

C **Read the conversation again. Underline two examples of Marie's interests and skills.**

D PAIRS **Have similar conversations. Ask and answer questions about two skills or interests you have and give an example for each one.**

WHAT DO YOU THINK?

GROUPS In the video, why do you think Kelly decides to place Marie in the marketing department? What other department might Marie be qualified to work in?

5 Noun clauses as objects

STUDY Noun Clauses as Objects

	Object
Let me show you	**where** you have to go.
This is	**how** we stock the shelves.
I don't know	**who** the new intern is.
Ask Mark	**when** the class is going to start.
Can you tell me	**what** happened?

Grammar Note

- A noun clause is a dependent clause that is used in the same way as a noun. Noun clauses are often used as objects.
- A noun clause contains a subject and a verb. The subject goes before the verb.
- A question changed to a noun clause is an embedded question. It uses statement word order: **What did you do?** ⟶ Please tell me **what you did.** / Can you tell me **what you did?**

PRACTICE

A **Circle the correct words.**

1. Tell me what (you enjoy) / do you enjoy doing.
2. Can you show me how **you fixed / did you fix** the photocopier?
3. I wonder who **is our new manager / our new manager is**.
4. I don't understand why **did he do / he did** that.
5. Do you know who **went / they went** to the convention?

B **Complete the sentences. Change the questions to noun clauses.**

1. *(When should I pick up my first paycheck?)*
   I'd like to know ____when I should pick up my first paycheck____.
2. *(What are we going to learn?)*
   Let me explain _____ in this class.
3. *(Who lives there?)*
   Can you tell me _____?
4. *(Where is the library?)*
   She's not sure _____.
5. *(How much do the sandwiches cost?)*
   I don't remember _____ in that café.

WHAT ABOUT YOU?

GROUPS Talk about places to go and things to do in the area near your school. Use the words from the box.

(I don't know where . . .   I'm not sure how . . .   Can you tell me when . . . ?)

A: *I don't know where the post office is.*
B: *It's on Bank Street, across from the supermarket.*

Paraphrase

GET READY

Kelly is reading an article about national parks. Have you ever been to a national park?

READ

🔊 **Listen and read the article on page 55. Which types of areas are part of the national park system?**

AFTER YOU READ

A **Read the Reading Skill. Read the article again. Underline the section of the text that the following paragraph paraphrases.**

You should go visit a national park if you've never been to one before. A lot of famous people worked hard to create national parks for everyone to enjoy.

> **Reading Skill**
>
> **Paraphrasing** is restating information in your own words. When you read, it's helpful to pause occasionally and try to restate information in your own words. If you can't restate the information, you probably haven't understood it very well.

B **Read the Reading Skill again. Rewrite the following sentences from the article in your own words. Use a separate piece of paper.**

John Muir was a naturalist who wanted to preserve nature for future generations. He found an ally in a tough young politician, Teddy Roosevelt.

C **Look at the chart in the article. What are the three most popular national parks in the United States?**

VOCABULARY STUDY Suffixes

> **Build Your Vocabulary**
>
> A **suffix** is a group of letters that you add to the end of a word to make a new word. To change some verbs to nouns, add the suffix *-(t)ion*, *-ation*, or *-ment*. For example: *invent + -ion* → *invention*.

Read the Build Your Vocabulary note. Then complete the chart with words from the article (they may be in a different form).

Verb	+ Suffix	Noun
act	-(t)ion	
_____		eruption
_____		location
protect		_____
_____	-ation	preservation
_____	-ment	development
		establishment

WHAT DO YOU THINK?

GROUPS According to the article, the national park system is one of the best ideas in U.S. history. Do you agree that it is a very good idea? Do you think it is a typically "American" idea? Why or why not?

> **ON THE WEB**
>
> For more information, go online and search "national parks." Find information about a national park and report back to the class.

NATIONAL PARKS

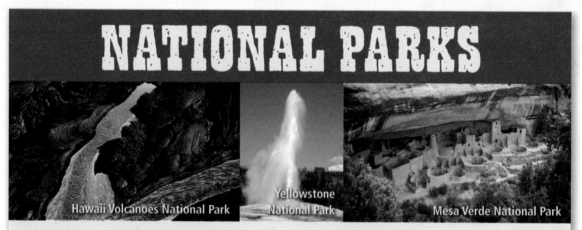

Hawaii Volcanoes National Park

Yellowstone National Park

Mesa Verde National Park

In Hawaii, lava flows slowly down a mountainside. It burns everything in its path. When it reaches the ocean, clouds of steam rise. Meanwhile, in Wyoming, a boiling hot geyser erupts about once an hour. It shoots a tower of water over 100 feet high. The smells of sulfur and pine trees mix in the dry mountain air. Finally, in Colorado, a rocky cliff looms above the canyon floor. If you look closely, you can see an ancient stone village under the cliff. Native Americans built the village over 700 years ago. What do these spectacular scenes have in common? They are all located in national parks.

A national park is an area that the government protects and allows people to visit. When people think of national parks, they think of nature. But monuments, battlefields, and even the White House are also part of the national park system. There is something for everyone. More than 250 million people visit national parks each year.

National parks are a relatively new concept. In the late 1800s, there were no protected natural areas. Americans cut down trees, mined, and built railroads all over the country. They didn't care about nature or the environment. But some people began to realize that natural areas needed protection.

Otherwise, the American wilderness would disappear forever.

John Muir was a naturalist who wanted to preserve nature for future generations. He found an ally in a tough young politician, Teddy Roosevelt. Roosevelt loved to hunt animals, but he also loved nature. So in 1903, Roosevelt and Muir traveled to Yosemite Valley in California. There they developed a plan to establish national parks. They thought that the government should buy beautiful natural areas. They should protect the resources, animals, and plants in these areas from harm. Everyone should be allowed to visit.

Roosevelt and Muir put their plan into action. Over the years, the national park system has expanded to include almost 400 protected areas. This concept has been called one of the most "American" ideas of our time. Pulitzer Prize winner Wallace Stegner said, "National parks are the best idea we ever had. Absolutely American, absolutely democratic, they reflect us at our best . . . "

So, if you've never been to a national park, visit one on your next vacation. Experience for yourself the wonders that Roosevelt, Muir, and others worked so hard to save for future generations.

5 Most Visited National Parks (2011)	
National Park	Park Visits
1. Great Smoky Mountains National Park (TN, NC)	9,008,830
2. Grand Canyon National Park (AZ)	4,298,178
3. Yosemite National Park (CA)	3,951,393
4. Yellowstone National Park (WY, MT, ID)	3,394,326
5. Rocky Mountain National Park (CO)	3,176,941

Source: National Park Service

7 Write about cause and effect

GET READY

Kelly is looking for ways that Traven Global staff can help people in the Miami community. She is reading a blog post about urban parks. Do you have parks in your neighborhood? Do you and your family use them?

STUDY THE MODEL

A **Skim the blog post. How does the writer feel about urban parks?**

www.hrinfosource.com

HRINFOSOURCE.com   ABOUT   TRENDS   WORKPLACE   WORKFORCE   BLOG   SEARCH

#COMMUNITY PROJECTS
#Urban Parks
by Nadine Bly on October 22, 2013 6 comments

Our company recently helped build Mavenwood Park, an urban park in the Mavenwood neighborhood of our city. We chose to get involved in urban parks for a number of reasons. Parks are beautiful and relaxing. They give people a way to escape from noise, crowds, and pollution. They can improve city life in many different ways. Let me tell you more about some of the ways our park has changed Mavenwood and made it a better place to live.

First of all, Mavenwood Park has improved public health in the neighborhood. Its playgrounds give children a place to have fun, be active, and lose weight. Both adults and children use its basketball courts and soccer fields to play games and exercise. Less physically active people take walks through the park.

Mavenwood Park has had another positive effect. It has made real estate values go up in the area. Because the park is a beautiful place, people want to live near it. As a consequence, houses and apartments near the park are worth more than ones that are far away.

Finally, the new park is making the local community stronger. The park provides pleasant open spaces that everyone can use. For this reason, it has made it easier for people to get to know their neighbors. People enjoy gathering in the park for organized social events such as picnics. But the park also offers different kinds of opportunities to keep people busy. Unemployed people can find decent jobs in the park. They weed flower beds, and they patrol the park to make it safer. They also help build new features in the park. In addition, the park offers programs and activities for teenagers. Thus, teenagers get into trouble less often because they have something productive to do with their time. People of any age can take part in park planning and management. For example, community members cultivate a garden in the park. They give away the fruits and vegetables they grow.

In conclusion, Mavenwood Park has affected the local community in very positive ways. This new park makes one thing very clear. There are good reasons to build as many new parks as we can in our cities.

B Read the Writing Tip. Then read the Writing Model again. Check [✓] the structure used in the Model.

☐ many causes, one effect
☐ one cause, many effects

C Read the Writing Tip and the Model again. Circle 4 logical connectors in the model.

D Look at the cause-and-effect chart the writer used and complete it with information from the Model.

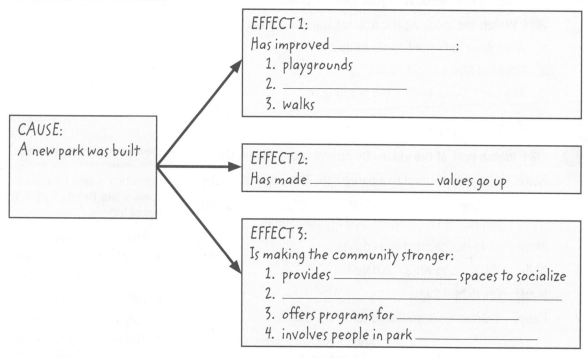

CAUSE:
A new park was built

EFFECT 1:
Has improved _____:
1. playgrounds
2. _____
3. walks

EFFECT 2:
Has made _____ values go up

EFFECT 3:
Is making the community stronger:
1. provides _____ spaces to socialize
2. _____
3. offers programs for _____
4. involves people in park _____

BEFORE YOU WRITE

A PAIRS Think about an event or situation that happened recently in your home or community. Make a list of the positive and/or negative effects that this has had on your family or community.

B You're going to write about one of the events or situations that you discussed in Exercise A. Complete a cause-and-effect chart to plan your essay. Use a separate piece of paper.

WRITE

Write a cause-and-effect essay. Review the Model and the Writing Tip. Use the ideas in your cause-and-effect chart. Use a separate piece of paper.

8 Give instructions

GET READY TO WATCH

Kelly and Marie are having a meeting in Kelly's office. What do you think Kelly is asking Marie to do?

WATCH

A ■◀ **Watch the video. Was your guess correct?**

B ■◀ **Watch the video again. Answer the questions.**

1. What does Kelly want Marie to do?

2. What did Marie forget to do?

3. Why can't Marie work in the mornings?

CONVERSATION

A ■◀ **Watch part of the video. Complete the conversation.**

Kelly: First, please read this paragraph. Then sign and date the line at the bottom. That _____ that you've read and understood the paragraph.

Marie: All right. . . . Here you go.

Kelly: You need to write the date here.

Marie: Oh, right. I forgot. Sorry.

Kelly: Thanks. Next, you need to fill out this _____ about your work schedule. Circle the days you're available on this line.

Marie: What should I write if I can only work in the afternoons? I have classes in the mornings.

Kelly: Just write the hours you're available underneath each day. We'll _____ your school schedule.

B PAIRS **Practice the conversation.**

C **Read the conversation again. Underline two places in the conversation where Kelly gives Marie instructions.**

D PAIRS **Have similar conversations. Give your partner instructions on how to do something.**

Pronunciation Note

Sometimes we pronounce vowels like the names of the vowel letters.

◀))) **Listen and repeat.**

A	/eɪ/	day	date
E	/i/	need	please
I	/aɪ/	line	write
O	/oʊ/	go	know
U	/(y)u/	use	afternoon

Note

GIVE INSTRUCTIONS
When you give instructions, it's a good idea to use simple imperative sentences. You can also use words like *first*, *next*, and *then* to help you sequence the instructions. This will make your instructions clear and easy to understand.

WHAT DO YOU THINK?

GROUPS In the video, Kelly gives Marie instructions. Are they clear? Why or why not? Think about the types of words or sentences she uses.

Sal Morales *Today*
Guess what! There's a job opening at Traven Global Coffee, where my old friend Eva works!

GET READY

Sal has found a few employment ads online.
Have you ever searched for a job online?

READ EMPLOYMENT ADS

Read the employment ads that Sal found. Answer the questions.

ACCOUNTANT

Company: Bellman Electronics
Location: Hollywood, FL 33024
Industry: Electronics
Job Type: Full-time
Years of Experience: Less than 1 year
Education Level: Bachelor's degree

SENIOR ACCOUNTANT

Company: Palladium Realty Partners
Location: Miami, FL 33131
Industry: Real Estate/Property Management
Job Type: Full-Time
Years of Experience: 10+
Education level: Master's degree in accounting, CPA (certified public accountant)

ACCOUNTANT

Company: Traven Global Coffee
Location: Miami, FL 33127
Industry: Food and beverage
Job Type: Full-time
Years of Experience: 3–5
Education Level: Bachelor's degree in accounting

Responsibilities:
- Prepare, review, and analyze financial statements, transactions, reports, budgets
- Ensure that financial reporting is done in accordance with accounting policies and procedures

Requirements:
- In-depth working knowledge of Excel, PeachTree
- Excellent communication skills
- Strong time management and organizational skills; detail oriented
- Able to work both independently and as a team player

1. What kinds of companies are offering the positions in the ads?

2. Which position requires the least amount of experience/education?

3. Which position requires the most experience/education?

4. Which skills does the Traven Global position require?

PUT YOUR IDEAS TO WORK

PAIRS Review Sal's self-assessment, job research, and goals from Units 1–3. Which job do you think matches his skills and experience the best? Which should he apply for?

ON THE WEB

Search for employment ads online. Find three ads that match your skills and interests and report back to the class.

GRAMMAR

See page 148 for your Grammar Review.

VOCABULARY See page 162 for the Unit 4 Vocabulary.

Vocabulary Learning Strategy: Write Personal Sentences

 A Choose 10 words or phrases from the list. In your notebook, use the words to write sentences about yourself or your opinions on something.

> I would like to work as an <u>intern</u> at a big company.
> I'm going to <u>renew</u> the lease on my apartment.

 B Underline the vocabulary words in your sentences in Exercise A.

SPELLING See page 162 for the Unit 4 Vocabulary.

CLASS Choose 10 words for a spelling test.

LISTENING PLUS

Watch each video. Write the story of Kelly's day on a separate piece of paper.

> Walt asks Kelly for help. He wants her to assign an intern to the marketing department.
> He needs help with the company website and his market research. . . .

NOW I CAN

PAIRS **See page 47 for the Unit 4 Goals.** Check ☑ the things you can do. Underline the things you want to study more. Then share your information with a partner.

> I can _____. I need more practice with _____.

5 Eva's Challenging Day

MY GOALS

- ☐ Troubleshoot a problem
- ☐ Evaluate marketing strategies
- ☐ Respond to criticism
- ☐ Offer to help
- ☐ Write a cover letter

Go to MyEnglishLab for more practice after each lesson.

Eva Vera

Eva   *Today*
Traffic was horrible this morning! I hope the rest of my day goes better . . .

1

Troubleshoot a problem

GET READY TO WATCH

Eva is trying to print some documents. What do you think is happening? How do you think Eva feels?

WATCH

A   ◀ Watch the video. Were your guesses correct?

B   ◀ Watch the video again. Answer the questions.

1. What is the first question Walt always asks when a machine doesn't work?
2. What does Walt think might be wrong with the paper?
3. What does Kelly give Eva?
4. Why is Eva upset at the end of the video?

CONVERSATION

A   ◀ Watch part of the video. Complete the conversation.

Walt: What's going on? Is there a problem with the printer?

Eva: Yeah. It must be _____. I've been trying to print out information for my sales presentation, and nothing is coming out.

Walt: Well, the first question I always ask in these situations is:

　　　Is the machine _____ in?

Eva: Yes, it is. I did check that!

Walt: Actually, the power light is on . . . so that can't be the problem. It could be out of paper, though.

Eva: I already checked all the paper trays. They're full.

Walt: Let's see, what else? . . . There might be a paper _____. . . . No, it doesn't look like that's the issue either.

B   PAIRS Practice the conversation.

C   Read the conversation again. Underline places where Eva and Walt try to troubleshoot the printer problem.

D   PAIRS Have your own conversations. Imagine that a machine or appliance isn't working. Troubleshoot the problem.

WHAT DO YOU THINK?

GROUPS In the video, Eva and Walt work together to troubleshoot the problem with the printer. Can you think of situations in which people worked together to troubleshoot problems in your home, school, or workplace? What happened?

GRAMMAR

Modals: Degrees of certainty

STUDY Modals: Degrees of Certainty

	Affirmative Statements	Negative Statements
99% sure		She **can't be** in her office. They **couldn't be** from Cuba.
95% sure	You **must like** seafood.	You **must not like** pork.
Less than 50% sure	He **may be** stuck in traffic.	He **may not get** here until 10 A.M.
	She **might know** how to fix the printer.	She **might not know** how to fix the computer.
	He **could be** on vacation.	

Grammar Note

- Use modals when you are not 100% certain if something is true.
- Use *must, have to,* or *have got to* if you are 95% certain: *He must like them. / He has got to like them.*

PRACTICE

A Circle the sentence that is closest in meaning to the first sentence.

1. That can't be the right answer.
   - **a.** That couldn't be the right answer.
   - **b.** That may not be the right answer.

2. She might need a new computer.
   - **a.** She must need a new computer.
   - **b.** She may need a new computer.

3. The car couldn't be out of gas.
   - **a.** The car can't be out of gas.
   - **b.** The car might not be out of gas.

4. He must be a good technician.
   - **a.** He may be a good technician.
   - **b.** He has got to be a good technician.

5. They may not live here.
   - **a.** They must not live here.
   - **b.** They might not live here.

B Complete the sentences. Use *can't, may not, might,* and *must* and the verbs from the box.

> be   have   know   make   ~~need~~

1. My camera ____*might need*____ a new battery, but I don't think so.
2. Marco was a mechanic for six years, so he _____ how to fix cars.
3. Gina _____ afraid of heights. She's a skydiver!
4. Min _____ a dish for the potluck, but she hates cooking, so she probably won't.
5. Yuri wants to come to the party, but he _____ time. He's busy these days.

WHAT ABOUT YOU?

PAIRS Talk about what *can't, could, may, might,* or *must* be true about each situation in the box.

> 1. A parked car's hood is open, and steam is rising from its engine.
> 2. There's a big package on your doorstep.
> 3. You haven't seen your neighbor for a long time.

3

Evaluate marketing strategies

GET READY

Eva is reading a marketing flyer about a fund-raising event for a local charity. Have you ever attended a fund-raising event? What was it raising money for?

PRACTICAL READING

A Read the marketing flyer. What kind of fund-raising event is it advertising?

FUNLAND PANCAKE BREAKFAST!!

A fund-raising event in aid of Support Florida Arts!
Help us keep art and music classes in our schools!

April 22, 2014
9 A.M. to 12 P.M.
Funland Amusement Park
16501 NE 15th Ave. • North Miami Beach, FL 33162

- Delicious pancakes, waffles, and hot and cold beverages will be served!
- Free rides on the Funland Ferris Wheel and other famous attractions!
- Local live bands and vendors!
- Raffle with great prizes! $5 per ticket!
- $10 donation requested.

Support Florida Arts is a community-based parent-teacher organization dedicated to saving art and music classes in our schools.

For further information or to volunteer for this event, please contact:
Mariana Vargas, Fund-raising Coordinator

fund-raising@supportfloridaarts.org

305-555-4565

B Read the flyer again. Then complete the sentences with the words from the box.

> charity   donation   fund-raising   raffle

1. The World Wildlife Fund is a well-known _____.
2. Some schools have to do a lot of _____ to pay for foreign language classes.
3. I made a _____ to the Food Bank for the Homeless.
4. Tickets for the _____ cost $10 each.

C Read the flyer again. Answer the questions.

1. Which organization is hosting the fund-raising event?

2. When and where is the event?

3. What kind of food will be served?

4. What kind of entertainment will be available?

5. How much money does the organization want people to donate?

6. What is the organization dedicated to doing?

7. Who can you contact if you want to help out at the event?

PRACTICAL LISTENING

A ◀)) **Nonprofit organizations and charities often use public service announcements, or PSAs, on the radio or TV to tell people about events they are organizing. Listen to the PSA. Answer the questions.**

1. What event is the PSA informing people about?

2. When and where is the event happening?

3. Which organization is planning the event, and what is its mission?

4. Why does the speaker say that art and music are essential for student success?

5. How can people register for the event?

6. What will people receive if they register?

B Compare the marketing flyer and the PSA. Which sentence do you think describes each marketing strategy? Complete the sentences with *flyer* or *PSA*.

The _____ tries to create a sense of urgency about the event/cause, and to make people feel like they must attend the event or help the cause.

The _____ tries to convince people to attend an event by focusing on the positive experiences people can have there.

WHAT DO YOU THINK?

GROUPS Review the flyer and the PSA. Which do you think is more convincing, and which event would you rather attend? Give reasons for your answer.

LESSON

Respond to criticism

GET READY TO WATCH

Gary has called Eva into his office to discuss a problem. Have you ever been criticized at work?

WATCH

◼◀ **Watch the video. Answer the questions.**

1. Why did Gary call Eva to his office?

2. What has Eva's team been doing, and why is it a problem?

3. What does Gary tell Eva to do?

4. What does Eva promise Gary?

CONVERSATION

A ◼◀ **Watch part of the video. Complete the conversation.**

Gary: Over the last month or so, your team has been offering customers a lot of discounts on our products.

Eva: Is that a problem? Discounts are a great sales
_____ .

Gary: Well, even though customers love discounts, we have to be careful about how we handle them.

Eva: I understand. Every time we offer a discount, we have to _____ up for the money lost somehow. But I thought we would be OK because we've been selling such large quantities.

Gary: Well, that's not the case. The discounts have definitely been impacting our bottom line recently. . . . Have the sales reps been checking with you before they offer discounts?

Eva: No, I've been leaving those decisions up to them.

Gary: I think you need to ask them to get your _____ before they offer discounts in the future.

Eva: OK, I will. I'm very sorry about this. I'll pass this information on to my team as soon as possible.

B PAIRS **Practice the conversation.**

C **Read the conversation again. Underline Eva's final response to Gary's criticism.**

D PAIRS **Have your own conversations. Switch roles.**

Student A: You are Student B's supervisor. Criticize Student B for a mistake he/she made.

Student B: Respond to the criticism.

> **Pronunciation Note**
>
> We break long sentences into shorter thought groups. Each thought group has at least one stressed word or syllable.
>
> ◀))) **Listen and repeat.**
>
> **Well,** / even though **cus**tomers love **dis**counts, / we have to be **care**ful / about how we **han**dle them.

> **Note**
>
> **RESPOND TO CRITICISM**
> When someone criticizes you, remain calm and listen before you respond. Make sure you understand the criticism. Decide if the criticism is fair or not. Then, if you did something wrong, acknowledge it and promise to fix the problem.

WHAT DO YOU THINK?

GROUPS In the video, Gary criticizes Eva for a mistake. Do you think Eva responds well to the criticism? Explain why or why not.

Adverb clauses: Concession

STUDY Adverb Clauses: Concession

Though **she works hard**,	she sometimes makes mistakes.
Although **we searched for hours**,	we couldn't find the keys.
We went to the beach last weekend	**even though** **there was a storm**.

Grammar Note

Adverb clauses are dependent clauses. They can show concession. They use words such as *though*, *although*, and *even though* to show that the information in the main clause is surprising or unexpected.

PRACTICE

 A Complete each sentence with *though*, *although*, or *even though* and a phrase from the box.

> she still forgot to sign the time sheet   they aren't technicians
> they didn't land the account   his boss criticized him unfairly
> he stayed late and finished his work   ~~you might not get it~~

1. You should apply for the job _though / although / even though you might not get it_ .

2. _____ the sales team offered the customer a hefty discount, _____

_____.

3. _____ he was very tired, _____.

4. _____ I reminded her, _____.

5. Tom and Ling fixed the printer _____.

6. Juan remained calm and listened carefully _____.

B Combine these sentences using *though*, *although*, or *even though*.
Use correct punctuation. Use a separate piece of paper.

1. I came late to the meeting. I didn't miss anything.

> _Though / Although / Even though I came late to the meeting, I didn't miss anything. OR_
> _I didn't miss anything though / although / even though I came late to the meeting._

2. He didn't call me back. I left three messages.   **4.** Her dress is still stained. She cleaned it.

3. I don't speak Spanish. I was born in Peru.   **5.** Ed's boss wasn't angry. He crashed the truck.

WHAT ABOUT YOU?

PAIRS Finish these sentences about yourself. Then tell your partner.

> **1.** Even though I _____ every day, I _____.
> **2.** Although it may be difficult, I believe I will _____.
> **3.** I can _____ though I can't _____.

Understand a sequence of events

Eva is reading an article about roller coasters. Do you enjoy riding on roller coasters?

◄))) **Listen and read the article. Why do people like to ride roller coasters?**

Roller Coasters: 300 Years of Thrills

You strap yourself in. The coaster gains speed. Suddenly, you're plunging down a steep slope. You're screaming . . . or laughing . . . or even crying. But you've rarely felt this exhilarated. Roller coasters have been thrilling us for over 300 years. They've changed a great deal since they were first invented, but one thing has remained the same. Roller coaster designers have always used the most up-to-date technology available to them to construct the most exciting rides they can.

The first versions of the roller coaster were made of ice and wood. The ice slide was a popular ride at winter fairs all over Russia in the 1700s. People rode a wooden sled or a block of ice, steering with a rope. Gravity pulled the riders down a steep slope. Later, an all-weather slide made of wood, wax, and rollers was designed. Accidents happened frequently on both types of slides. To make the rides less dangerous, designers began to build roller coasters on tracks.

In the United States, the earliest roller coaster started out as a railroad in Pennsylvania. A mining company used the Mauch Chunk Switchback Railway to roll mining carts full of coal downhill. In the 1870s, the Mauch Chunk began to permit passengers to ride the mining carts. In the decades that followed, roller coaster development exploded.

"Flying" roller coaster

Soon "sit down" and "stand up" wooden coasters became a common feature at amusement parks.

Today, roller coasters have spread all over the world. Traditional wooden coasters still have their fans, but most coasters are now made of steel. Computer technology generates the speed and turns. In "suspended" roller coasters, riders sit in cars hanging from the track. In "flying" coasters, riders lie down in the cars, "flying" below the track. Finally, in "fourth dimension" coasters, riders sit on either side of the track. The seats . . . and the riders in them . . . spin around the track as they move.

Designers around the world try to outdo each other by building bigger, faster, and more intense rides. For example, the recently constructed Formula Rossa in Abu Dhabi can reach over 149 miles per hour! Some creative designers develop truly unique experiences for their riders. The Vanish in Japan unexpectedly dives into an underwater tunnel. Meanwhile, the interactive Shweeb in New Zealand lets you control your own ride. You lie in a see-through pod and pedal yourself through the twists and turns.

So the next time you're looking for excitement, hop on a roller coaster. Whatever kind of coaster you ride, it's sure to be a thrilling experience!

AFTER YOU READ

A Read the Reading Skill. Read the article again. Circle all the dates and phrases such as *first*, *next*, *later*, *soon*, *recently*, and *finally*.

B Read the Reading Skill and the article again. Number the following events in the order they occurred (*1* to *6*).

_____ Invention of "flying" roller coasters

_____ Invention of ice slides

_____ Invention of "stand-up" wooden coasters

_____ Construction of Formula Rossa

_____ Invention of roller coasters on tracks

_____ The Mauch Chunk Railway permits passengers on mining cars

VOCABULARY STUDY Word Families

Build Your Vocabulary

A **word family** is a group of words that share a common root, to which different prefixes and suffixes are added. For example: From the root *act* you can form the nouns *actor* and *action*, the verbs *act* and *react*, the adjective *active*, and the adverb *actively*.

Read the Build Your Vocabulary note. Complete items 1–6 with words from the article. Then complete items 7–8. For item 8, try to think of your own example.

Root	Noun	Verb	Adjective
1. *rid*	rider, ride		—
2. *danger*	danger	endanger	
3. *thrill*	thrill		thrilling
4. *creat*	creation	create	
5. *interact*	interaction	interact	
6. *excit*		excite	exciting
7. *amaz*	amazement		
8.			

WHAT DO YOU THINK?

GROUPS Which of the roller coasters mentioned in the article sound most appealing? Is there a kind of roller coaster that you wish roller coaster designers could invent? Describe it.

Write about steps in a process

GET READY

Eva is reading a memo about how to operate the new security system at the Traven Global office. Have you ever had to use a security system or alarm at home or work?

STUDY THE MODEL

A **Read the memo. Are the instructions easy to understand? Why or why not?**

MEMO

To: All Traven Global managers
From: Bob Janek, Facilities manager
Date: Friday, February 15, 2014
Subject: Operating instructions for new security system

Dear Managers,

Our new security system has finally been installed. It is now operational. Here are some basic instructions on how to operate the system. For security reasons, please don't share these instructions with others. They are for authorized staff members only.

Instructions for operating the security system:

Before you turn on or "arm" the system at the end of the work day, you need to do the following. First, make sure you are the last person in the building. Then make sure that all doors and windows are closed and locked. Of course, the door you will exit from should be closed, but not locked.

To arm the system, press the "Doors+windows" button on the alarm display. Then enter the four-digit security code **5134**. As soon as you do that, press "motions." This will arm the motion detector. You will hear two beeps every five seconds while you exit the building. Exit and lock the door behind you. The beeps will continue for one minute. Then they will stop automatically.

Troubleshooting problems:

a. If you press the "Doors+windows" button and there is an open door or window, you will hear beeps and see a message on the display. The message will tell you which door or window is open. At this time, you must press "Disarm" and enter the security code to turn off the system. As soon as you do that, the beeping will stop. After you have turned off the system, go and lock the open door or window. Then set the alarm again.

b. If you have armed the system, but realize that you have forgotten something in your office, you should disarm the system. Do not try to run back to your office. You will not have time, and the alarm system will go off. Just disarm the system by pressing "Disarm" and entering the security code. Go back to your office for your forgotten item. When you are ready to leave, arm the system again.

B Read the Writing Tip. Read the Model again. Underline the time clauses and *if* clauses.

C Look at the flowchart the writer used and complete it with information from the Model.

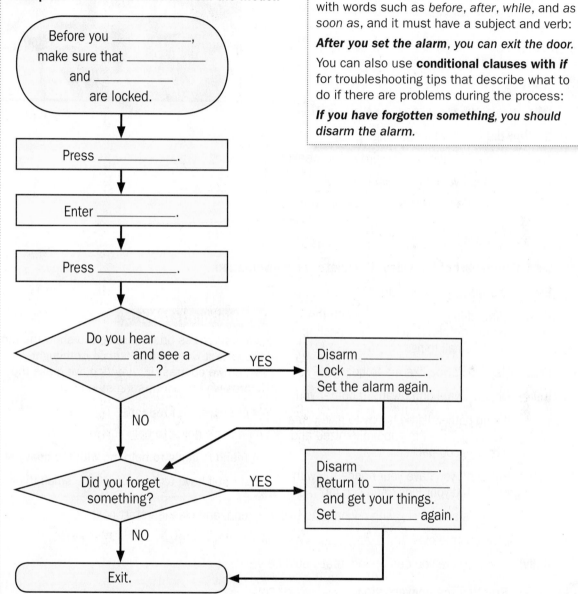

Before you _____, make sure that _____ and _____ are locked.

↓

Press _____.

↓

Enter _____.

↓

Press _____.

↓

Do you hear _____ and see a _____? — **YES** → Disarm _____. Lock _____. Set the alarm again.

NO ↓

Did you forget something? — **YES** → Disarm _____. Return to _____ and get your things. Set _____ again.

NO ↓

Exit.

BEFORE YOU WRITE

A **PAIRS** Think about something that you did at home, school, or work that required you to follow steps in a process. Make a list of steps you followed to complete the task. Try to include troubleshooting tips.

B You're going to write about steps in a process. Write about the steps you discussed in Exercise A. Create a flowchart to plan your paragraphs. Use a separate piece of paper.

WRITE

Write about steps in a process. Review the Model and the Writing Tip. Use the ideas in your flowchart. Use a separate piece of paper.

GET READY TO WATCH

Eva and Kelly are leaving work at the end of the day. What do coworkers usually talk about when they leave work?

WATCH

🎬 **Watch the video. Answer the questions.**

1. Why did Eva have a challenging day?
2. Why isn't Kelly looking forward to the weekend?
3. What does Eva offer to help Kelly do?
4. How does Kelly describe her new place to live?

CONVERSATION

A 🎬 **Watch part of the video. Complete the conversation.**

Eva: Is anyone going to help you _____?

Kelly: A friend is going to help me with the heavy stuff. But I still have to pack up all the small things.

Eva: Hey, would you like me to help you?

Kelly: Oh, no, Eva. I don't want to bother you.

Eva: It's no bother. I'd be happy to give you a _____. I'm super-organized and a really good packer.

Kelly: But don't you have your hands full with work? And your kids? And school?

Eva: The girls are staying with my parents this weekend, and classes start next week.

I could come over first _____.

Kelly: If you're sure you don't mind, that would be great.

> ### Pronunciation Note
>
> We use stress and intonation to show the most important word in a sentence or thought group. When we contrast information, we make the words we are contrasting stand out.
>
> 🔊 **Listen and repeat.**
>
> Is anyone going to help you **move**?
>
> A friend is going to help me with the **heavy** stuff.
>
> But I still have to pack up all the **small** things.

B **PAIRS** **Practice the conversation.**

C **Read the conversation again. Underline three different ways in which Eva offers to help.**

D **PAIRS** **Have similar conversations. Switch roles.**

Student A: Talk about something you have to do.

Student B: Offer to help. Explain how you can help.

WHAT DO YOU THINK?

GROUPS Do you think Eva is sincere in her offer to help Kelly? How do you know when someone makes a sincere offer? Why do you think people sometimes make offers, but they don't really mean it?

Sal Morales   *Today*
I'm about to apply for
the job at Traven Global.
Wish me luck!

GET READY

Sal is applying for an accounting position. He has written a cover letter to send to Traven Global. Have you ever written a cover letter?

READ A COVER LETTER

A **Read Sal's cover letter. Answer the questions.**

Kelly Chen
Human Resources
Traven Global Coffee, Inc.
3818 N. Miami Ave.
Miami, FL 33127

Sal Morales
3105 W. 2nd Ave
Hialeah, FL 33014
305-555-3158
salmorales@gmail.com

March 30, 2014

Dear Ms. Chen,

    I saw your advertisement for the accounting position on jobmarket.com last week. I am writing to express my interest in this position. I am enclosing my résumé for your perusal. I am also sending a reference from one of your staff members, Eva Vera.

    I am confident that I am a highly qualified candidate for this position. For the past five years, I've been employed as an accountant at Julio's Best Automotive Shop. Among other duties, I've prepared, reviewed, and analyzed financial statements, reports, and budgets. I worked closely with the owner of the company to reduce costs and increase profits. Additionally, I have a bachelor's degree in accounting from the University of Miami. I am proficient in Excel, QuickBooks, and PeachTree. I possess excellent communication, time management, and organizational skills.

    I would welcome the opportunity to interview with you for this position. Please feel free to contact me if you need any further information. Thank you for your consideration. I look forward to hearing from you soon.

Sincerely,
Sal Morales

1. Which documents is Sal sending to Kelly?

2. Who wrote a reference for Sal?

3. What does Sal ask for at the end the letter?

B See page 59 for the Traven Global Coffee accountant ad. **Underline the sentences in the cover letter in which Sal shows that he can handle the responsibilities and requirements mentioned in the ad.**

PUT YOUR IDEAS TO WORK

A **Think of a job that you want to apply for. Write a cover letter to the HR manager of the company. Use Sal's cover letter as a model.**

B PAIRS **Compare your cover letter with your partner's. Do you think the HR managers will give you interviews? If necessary, suggest changes or improvements.**

GRAMMAR

See page 149 for your Grammar Review.

VOCABULARY See page 162 for the Unit 5 Vocabulary.

Vocabulary Learning Strategy: Group by Function

 A **Choose words from the list and add them to these sentences.**

Words I use when I . . .

• Troubleshoot problems with machines or appliances: _jam,_____

_____

• Give money to those in need: _charity,_____

• Apply for a job: _candidate,_____

B **Underline 5 words from Exercise A. Write a sentence with each word.**

SPELLING See page 162 for the Unit 5 Vocabulary.

CLASS Choose 10 words for a spelling test.

LISTENING PLUS

Watch each video. Write the story of Eva's day on a separate piece of paper.

> _Eva has a problem printing out some documents at work. Walt tries to help her troubleshoot the problem. . . ._

NOW I CAN

PAIRS See page 61 for the Unit 5 Goals. Check ☑ the things you can do.
Underline the things you want to study more. Then share your information
with a partner.

I can _____. I need more practice with _____.

6 Walt Has an Idea

MY GOALS

- ☐ Propose an idea
- ☐ Interpret directions
- ☐ Demonstrate technology skills
- ☐ Compromise
- ☐ Prepare a résumé

Go to MyEnglishLab for more practice after each lesson.

Walt Soares

Walt *Today*
I have a great idea for an online contest. I hope my boss likes it!

75

1 Propose an idea

 ## GET READY TO WATCH

Walt is telling Gary about an idea he has.
Have you ever proposed an idea to your boss?
How did you feel?

WATCH

◼◀ **Watch the video. Answer the questions.**

1. What is Walt's idea?

2. What does Gary think will be expensive?

3. What does Gary want Walt to do at 2:00 P.M.?

4. How does Walt feel about doing what Gary wants?

CONVERSATION

A ◼◀ **Watch part of the video. Complete the conversation.**

Walt: What if we had _____ for customers
who place online orders?

Gary: How would it work?

Walt: Well, this is what I'm thinking. Every time a customer
places an order, a series of photos pops up on
the screen.

Gary: Photos of what?

Walt: _____ photos from coffee-producing
countries like Costa Rica, Ethiopia, Brazil. . . . The
customer has to identify the country where each
photo was taken.

Gary: And what happens then?

Walt: The people who identify the photos correctly will be "finalists" in the contest.

One of them will win an _____ to a coffee-producing country.

Pronunciation Note

Most two-syllable nouns are
stressed on the first syllable.
Two-syllable verbs are often
stressed on the second syllable.

◀)) **Listen and repeat.**

product   **con**test   **na**ture

pro**pose**   pre**pare**   in**clude**

B PAIRS **Practice the conversation.**

C **Read the conversation again. Underline 3 sentences in which Walt gives details
about the idea he is proposing.**

D PAIRS **Think of an idea that you would like to propose. Write a few details about
the idea. Then have your own conversations.**
Student A: Propose an idea.
Student B: Ask for more details.

WHAT DO YOU THINK?

GROUPS In the video, Walt proposes an idea. Does it sound like a good one?
Why or why not? What other kinds of contests could the Traven Global website offer?

Adjective clauses

STUDY Adjective Clauses

Pronoun Used as Subject
The man **who lives** next door came over yesterday.
The company **that makes** this coffee is small.
Let's go to the café **which is** on 14ᵗʰ Street.

Pronoun Used as Object
The woman **who(m) I spoke** to was the receptionist.
The presentation **that we saw** was about sales.
I liked the idea **which he proposed**.

Grammar Note

- An adjective clause is a dependent clause that describes, identifies, or gives more information about a noun.
- Use the relative pronouns *who(m)* for people, *which* for things, and *that* for both people and things.
- Relative pronouns used as subjects cannot be left out of adjective clauses: ~~The man lives next door came over yesterday.~~
  Relative pronouns used as objects are often left out:
  I liked the idea he proposed.

PRACTICE

A **Complete the sentences with *who(m)*, *that*, or *which*. More than one answer may be possible.**

1. Many companies try to create websites ___*that* OR *which*___ will attract customers.

2. People _____ visit websites can sometimes participate in contests.

3. Contestants can win prizes _____ include money, free gifts, or coupons.

4. Mark took part in a contest _____ he entered on a website.

5. The free trip _____ he won in the contest was a lot of fun.

6. He met some people on the trip _____ he liked a lot.

B **Combine the two sentences. Change the second sentence to an adjective clause. Use a separate piece of paper.**

1. I liked the blog. You posted it on the website.

> I liked the blog that you posted on the website. OR I liked the blog which you posted on the website. OR I liked the blog you posted on the website.

2. She suggested an idea. The idea could solve all the company's problems.

3. Those are the two people. They won the contest.

4. They gave the job to the man. Olivia recommended him.

5. Jim is looking forward to the business trip. He's taking a business trip next month.

WHAT ABOUT YOU?

PAIRS Make 4 sentences using adjective clauses from the box.
Talk about someone or something . . .

who has helped you	who(m) you love and respect	that is exciting
that you would like to help	which you would like to buy	

A person whom I love and respect is my grandmother.

Interpret directions

GET READY

Walt is going to use a computer to give a presentation. Have you ever used a computer to give a presentation in class or at work?

PRACTICAL READING

A **Skim the directions. What do they explain how to do?**

C1

Connecting your laptop to a projector:

You will need the following: a laptop computer, a laptop power cord, a video cable (or monitor cable), a projector, and an XXX cord (for audio). Note that different types of laptops may require different equipment. Examine the video and audio ports on the side of your laptop to make sure your video cable and XXX cord match. If they do not, you will need to acquire the correct cable and/or cord before proceeding with the setup instructions below.

Follow these instructions:

1. Turn the projector on.
2. Connect the video cable to the laptop's video port (on most laptops, a blue-colored port that is "D" shaped).
3. Connect the video cable to the projector's video port.
4. If using audio, plug the XXX cord into your laptop's "audio out" port. Then connect the XXX cord to the projector. If the sound system is separate from the projector, connect it to that sound system.
5. Make sure that the laptop power cord is plugged into a wall socket or an extension cord. This will ensure that your laptop battery will not run low and shut down in the middle of your presentation.
6. Turn on the laptop and wait a minute or two. Your laptop will probably automatically recognize the projector. If it does not, try one of the following steps:
    a) Go to the Control Panel on your laptop, and click on the Settings button. In the Settings window, select the projector as your display monitor.
    b) Hold down the Function (Fn) key on your keyboard while pressing the F7 key. (On some computers, you may have to press the F4, F5, or F8 key instead.)
7. Your laptop may automatically download software from the projector. This enables your laptop to work with the projector.
8. You may be asked if you want to display your presentation on the screen only, or on both the screen and your laptop. Select the way you would like the presentation to appear.
9. Open up your presentation document.
10. Go to the first slide and make sure that the picture shows up on the screen. If necessary, check the audio as well.
11. Once you have made sure that everything is ready to go, close the lid of your laptop. When you are ready to start your presentation, simply open the lid and begin.

B **Read the directions more carefully. Complete the sentences with words from the box.**

> display   projector   port   video cable   wall socket

1. A _____ enables you to _____ your presentation slides on a large screen.

2. We used a _____ to connect the laptop to the projector.

3. If your laptop battery is low, you need to plug your laptop into a _____.

4. Plug the XXX cord into the audio _____ on your laptop.

C **Read the directions again. Number the steps in the correct order (1 to 7).**

_____ Start the slideshow to make sure that the picture shows up on the big screen.

_____ On your laptop, click on your presentation document to open the slideshow.

_____ Choose if you want to see your presentation on your laptop and the big screen, or only on the big screen.

_____ Plug in your laptop power cord, and then turn on your laptop.

_____ Give your laptop time to connect to the projector.

_____ Check to see that your ports match your cables and cords.

_____ If necessary, hold down the Fn key while pressing on the F7 key.

D PAIRS **Compare your answers from Exercise C. Then practice giving the instructions in your own words.**

PRACTICAL LISTENING

◀)) **Listen to the instructions. Answer the questions.**

1. What number do you press to get instructions in English?

2. What do the instructions tell you how to do?

3. How many digits do you need to have in a PIN?

4. What do you do after you record your new PIN?

5. What do you do if you don't want to record a personal greeting?

6. If you aren't happy with a recording and want to rerecord it, what do you do?

7. What can you do if you need more tips and instructions?

WHAT DO YOU THINK?

GROUPS Was it easier to understand the written instructions or the audio instructions? Give reasons for your answer.

4 Demonstrate technology skills

GET READY TO WATCH

Walt and Marie are in the conference room before Walt's presentation. What do you think they are trying to do?

WATCH

A 📹 **Watch the video. Was your guess correct?**

B 📹 **Watch the video again. Answer the questions.**

1. When will the presentation start?

2. What do Marie and Walt connect to Walt's laptop?

3. What will Marie do while Walt is talking during the presentation?

4. Why does Walt leave the room at the end of the video?

CONVERSATION

A 📹 **Watch part of the video. Complete the conversation.**

Walt: Hey, Marie. The presentation starts in five minutes. Do we have everything we need?

Marie: I think so. The _____ is on the table, and here's the cable. Do you have your laptop?

Walt: Yes. Here you go.

Marie: Thanks. This cable has to be hooked up to the video _____ on your laptop. Where is it?

Walt: Here, I've got it. . . . Uh-oh. It's not going in!

Marie: Actually, I think it's just _____.

Walt: Oh, OK . . . There we go.

Marie: OK, I think we're all set!

> **Pronunciation Note**
>
> To say /ð/, the *th* sound in *this*, put your tongue between your teeth and use your voice.
> To say /θ/, the *th* sound in *think*, put your tongue between your teeth and do not use your voice.
>
> 🔊 **Listen and repeat.**
>
> | /ð/ | this | there |
> |---|---|---|
> | /θ/ | think | thanks |

B PAIRS **Practice the conversation.**

C Read the conversation again. Underline the parts of the conversation where Walt and Marie show their technology skills.

D PAIRS **Have you had to demonstrate your technology skills by setting up a device, appliance, or machine recently? Think about the steps you took. Then have your own conversations. Imagine you are setting up a new device, appliance, or machine together.**

WHAT DO YOU THINK?

GROUPS In the video, Walt and Marie prepare for Walt's presentation on short notice. Do they do a good job? What could they do better?

GRAMMAR

Passive voice with modals

STUDY Passive Voice with Modals

	Modal	*be*	Past Participle	
The machine	**has to**	be	**set up**	properly.
The computer	**must**	be	**turned off**	at the end of the day.
The package	**should**	be	**sent**	as soon as possible.
Tickets	**can't**	be	**sold**	until July 14.
All employees	**will**	be	**told**	about the new rule.

> **Grammar Note**
>
> You can use the following modals in present passive forms: *may, can, will, should, ought to, must, have to, had better,* and *be supposed to.*

PRACTICE

A **Complete the sentences with the passive voice form of the verbs.**

1. Projectors _____ *can be used* _____ to give presentations.
   _{can / use}

   Your laptop _____ to the projector with this cord.
   _{must / connect}

2. At night, photos _____ with a flash.
   _{should / take}

3. Her supervisor _____ that she is taking time off.
   _{has to / tell}

   Her coworkers _____, too.
   _{ought to / inform}

4. The new software _____ soon. The staff
   _{will / introduce}

   _____ how to use it.
   _{had better / teach}

B **Complete the passive sentences with the verbs from the box and the modals.**

> announce   build   change   ~~encourage~~   open

1. Customers _____ *ought to be encouraged* _____ to visit the website more often.
   _{ought to}

2. That policy _____ because it doesn't make sense.
   _{should}

3. The winners _____ next Friday.
   _{will}

4. The supermarket's doors _____ at 8 A.M.
   _{must}

5. A new school _____ in this neighborhood next year.
   _{may}

WHAT ABOUT YOU?

PAIRS What do you think should be done about the economy? The environment? The schools? Make passive sentences with modals.

I think more jobs have to be created because too many people are unemployed.

6 Identify a writer's purpose

GET READY

Walt is reading an article about an interesting neighborhood. What is an interesting neighborhood that people like to visit in your area?

READ

🔊)) **Listen and read the article. Where is Little Havana?**

Little Havana: A Unique Cultural Experience

Most visitors to Miami come for the beautiful beaches, great shopping, and sports events. But Miami is also an international city that dances to a different beat. The city is home to people from all over South America. As such, it offers unique opportunities to enjoy Latin culture. One of the best ways to get to know Miami is by visiting Little Havana.

Located west of downtown Miami, Little Havana is a place full of music, art . . . and delicious food. The main street is called *Calle Ocho* (Southwest Eighth Street). There, you'll find grocery stores that offer Latino delicacies, fresh fruit markets, and juice shops. You'll also find famous restaurants where you can savor typical Cuban dishes like fried plantains, black beans, and *ropa vieja* ("old clothes," or shredded beef). Of course, you'll want to sample a *cafecito*, a small cup of strong Cuban coffee.

Little Havana is also a good place to explore Cuban history and culture. The Cuban Memorial Plaza celebrates important events in Cuban history, while the Walkway of the Stars honors Cuban entertainers. Near the center of Little Havana is Maximo Gomez Park, also known as Domino Park. It is named for the many domino players who congregate in the park every day. It's fun to watch the games and listen to the clatter of dominoes. And don't forget to check out the various cigar shops, where employees roll cigars by hand in the traditional way.

It's important to keep in mind, though, that Little Havana is not just Cuban. It's about all things Latino. Visitors to Little Havana are often blown away by the variety of cultural experiences they can enjoy. For example, Cultural Fridays (*Viernes Culturales*) is a free evening street festival. It should be at the top of your Miami must-do list. When you go, be ready to let loose and enjoy yourself! The streets are closed to traffic, and there is live music. If you like to dance, you can join a free salsa or tango class. The food choices are endless. If art is your passion, you can amble through the many art galleries and artist studios. Interested in architecture? Join a local guide for a free tour of Little Havana at 7 P.M.

If you take the time to step into Little Havana, you will see a side of Miami that many tourists miss. Come and join the celebration of cultures. I guarantee that you will want to come back.

Writers usually write texts for particular reasons. For example, the writer may want to tell a story, describe a situation, give an opinion, or offer a recommendation. When you read, try to **identify the writer's purpose**. This will help you understand the material.

A **Read the Reading Skill. Read the article again. Circle the writer's main purpose in writing the article.**

a. To describe Little Havana's architecture   **b.** To explain Little Havana's history

c. To encourage people to visit Little Havana   **d.** To inform people about Cuban food

B **PAIRS** **Read the Reading Skill and the article again. Compare your answers from Exercise A. Then identify a few sentences in the article that you think show the writer's purpose.**

C **Look at the map. Then complete the sentences about each number on the map.**

1. The Cuban Memorial Plaza is at the corner of _____ and _____.

2. The "Walkway of the Stars" is a sidewalk along _____ with stars for famous entertainers.

3. Domino Park is on _____ between _____ and _____.

VOCABULARY STUDY Context Clues

Build Your Vocabulary

When you come across new words while reading, you can use **context clues** to guess their meanings. *Context* means the words that come before or after a word in a sentence.

Read the Build Your Vocabulary note. Try to guess the meanings of the words in the box. Then find and underline each of the words in the article. Read each word in its context. Write the words next to their definitions.

> amble   blown away   clatter   congregate   savor

_____ = eat or enjoy slowly

_____ = gather

_____ = surprised

_____ = the loud noise made by things hitting together

_____ = walk slowly

WHAT DO YOU THINK?

GROUPS According to the article, Little Havana is a great place to visit. From what you know about the area, do you agree? What would you like to do there?

ON THE WEB

For more information, go online and search "Little Havana, Miami." Find out two more things people can do in Little Havana. Share them with the class.

7

Write a description

Walt is reading an email from a coworker who is in Rio de Janeiro, Brazil.
What do you know about Rio de Janeiro?

A **Read the email. How does the writer feel about Rio de Janeiro?**

From: Trish Fallon (tfallon@tgc.com)
Sent: Friday, April 15, 2014, 8:30 P.M.
To: Walt Soares (wsoares@tgc.com)
Subject: Brazil trip update

Hi, Walt.

I just wanted to give you an update on my business trip to Brazil. So far,
everything has been great. My meetings with the reps went really well—I'll send
you a detailed report in a couple of days. They've gone to a lot of trouble to show
me a good time, too!

Now I'm spending a few vacation days in Rio de Janeiro before I head back to
Miami on Sunday. What a city! This place has it all: beautiful scenery, great
weather, friendly people, and fascinating attractions. My hotel is in Zona Sul, right
on the Copacabana. There's a reason the Copacabana is one of the most famous
beaches in the world. First of all, it's the biggest beach I've ever seen, especially
in the middle of a city! It has sparkling sand, huge waves, and crowds of
gorgeous people talking in Portuguese. I spend a couple of hours there every
day, lying on a beach towel and soaking up the hot sun.

There are also great restaurants in this city, and I've been eating delicious meals
every night. My favorite so far has been "feijoada." It's a very filling black bean
stew, and it smells unbelievably good. I also loved "moqueca de peixe," which
is a rich fish stew made with coconut. And they serve "pao de quiejo," a kind
of tasty cheese bread, with every meal. I think I've gained 10 pounds in the last
week. After dinner, I usually listen to some music in a club. I'm crazy about
bossa nova . . . listening to it makes me feel so relaxed.

Yesterday, I took a cable car to the top of Sugarloaf Mountain. I'm sure you've
seen pictures of it: It looks like a big loaf of bread (or sugar) sticking out of the
sea. From the top, you get a great view of most of Rio . . . the beaches, the
modern highrise buildings, and the tiny boats in the harbor far below. There are
steep hills and mountains all over the city, and one of them has a huge statue on
top of it called the Corcovado. I stayed until the sun set, and it was spectacular.

It's going to be hard to leave this place, but I'm looking forward to seeing you soon!

Take care,

Trish

B **Read the Writing Tip. Then read the Model again. Underline examples of the following details in the Model.**

a. a sensory detail about how something looks

b. a sensory detail about how something sounds

c. a sensory detail about how something smells

d. a sensory detail about how something tastes

e. a sensory detail about how something feels

C **Look at the "flower" graphic organizer the writer used and complete it with information from the Model.**

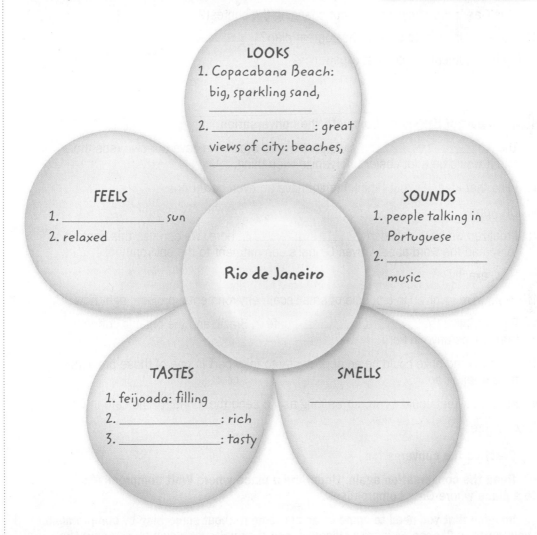

LOOKS
1. Copacabana Beach: big, sparkling sand, _____
2. _____: great views of city: beaches, _____

FEELS
1. _____ sun
2. relaxed

SOUNDS
1. people talking in Portuguese
2. _____ music

Rio de Janeiro

TASTES
1. feijoada: filling
2. _____: rich
3. _____: tasty

SMELLS
_____

BEFORE YOU WRITE

You're going to write a description of a place. It can be somewhere you've visited or a place where you spend a lot of time. Use a "flower" graphic organizer to plan your description, and include sensory details. Use a separate piece of paper.

WRITE

Write a description of a place. Review the Model and the Writing Tip. Use the ideas in your "flower" graphic organizer to write your description.

8 Compromise

GET READY TO WATCH

Walt and Gary are coming to a compromise on Walt's proposal. What is a compromise? Do you try to compromise when you discuss issues with people?

WATCH

■◀ **Watch the video. Answer the questions.**

1. What is Gary's first suggestion about changing the contest?

2. How does Walt want to change the contest plan?

3. Who will document the contest experience?

CONVERSATION

A ■◀ **Watch part of the video. Complete the conversation.**

Gary: The _____ should be a trip to Brazil. We have our own reps there, and it would be a lot easier to organize everything.

Walt: I like that idea . . . but I think I might have an even better one.

Gary: Oh, yeah?

Walt: I realized we have a golden _____ here. We can use this contest to spread the word about Traven Global's commitment to the environment.

Gary: How, exactly?

Walt: Well, we're involved in a couple of small-scale environmental projects right now . . .

Gary: Right . . . like the _____ café in Brazil, and the organic coffee farm cooperative in Peru.

Walt: So the grand prize could be an opportunity to take part in one of those projects for a week or so.

Gary: Hmm . . . that could work . . . as long as we send the winner to the café in Brazil!

Walt: OK, sure.

B PAIRS **Practice the conversation.**

C PAIRS **Read the conversation again. Underline a place where Walt compromises. Circle a place where Gary compromises.**

D PAIRS **Imagine that you need to come to an agreement about something by compromising with your partner. Choose an issue to discuss, and then write your own ideas about the issue. Then have your own conversations. Come to an agreement through compromise.**

WHAT DO YOU THINK?

GROUPS In the video, Gary and Walt want customers to know that Traven Global is helping people and the environment in coffee-producing countries. Why?

Sal Morales *Today*
I've just updated my résumé! New job, here I come!

GET READY

Sal is going to send his résumé to companies, along with his cover letter.
Have you ever prepared a résumé? What information is important to include?

READ A RÉSUMÉ

A **Read Sal's résumé. Answer the questions.**

> ### Sal Morales
> 3105 W. 2nd Ave., Hialeah, FL 33014
> Cell phone: 305-555-3158
> Email: salmorales@gimail.com
>
> **OBJECTIVE**
> I am seeking an accountant position in a small, fast-growing company with leadership training opportunities.
>
> **WORK EXPERIENCE**
> **Accountant, Julio's Best Automotive Shop, North Miami, FL**
> June 2009 – April 2014
> Full-time accounting position at small business with 30 employees. Prepared, reviewed, and analyzed financial reports and budgets in accordance with company policies. Contributed to the reduction of expenses and increase in profits.
>
> **Bookkeeping Assistant, Green Bakery Supply Systems, Hialeah, FL**
> Sept. 2007–May 2009
> Part-time position in a large independently owned bakery supply company. Assisted in preparation of payroll and expense documentation required for contracts with local bakeries and restaurants.
>
> **EDUCATION**
> University of Miami, Miami, FL
> Bachelor's degree in Accounting, May 2009, GPA: 3.60
>
> **COMPUTER SKILLS**
> Proficient in Excel, Microsoft Word, QuickBooks, and PeachTree

1. How long did Sal work at the automotive shop? What did he do there?

2. When did Sal graduate from college? What was his grade point average?

3. What was Sal doing while he was attending college?

4. What computer programs is he knowledgeable about?

B PAIRS See page 73 for Sal's cover letter. **Which information does Sal include in both the résumé and the cover letter? Why do you think he chose to include it in both places?**

PUT YOUR IDEAS TO WORK

A **Make a time line of your work and education in the last several years. Use that information to prepare your résumé. Use Sal's résumé as a model.**

B PAIRS **Show your résumé to your partner. Discuss changes or improvements.**

GRAMMAR

See page 150 for your Grammar Review.

VOCABULARY See page 162 for the Unit 6 Vocabulary.

Vocabulary Learning Strategy: Describe Objects Around You

A Imagine that you are in a computer lab, office, or classroom. Look at the objects around you. Write words from the list that describe the objects you see.

a cable,

B Circle 5 words in Exercise A. Write a sentence for each word.

SPELLING See page 162 for the Unit 6 Vocabulary.

CLASS Choose 10 words for a spelling test.

LISTENING PLUS

Watch each video. Write the story of Walt's day on a separate piece of paper.

Walt proposes an idea to Gary. He wants to have an online contest to get people to order more products from the Traven Global website. . . .

NOW I CAN

PAIRS See page 75 for the Unit 6 Goals. Check ☑ the things you can do. Underline the things you want to study more. Then share your information with your partner.

I can ____. I need more practice with ____.

7 Matt Focuses on Safety

MY GOALS

☐ Describe an accident

☐ Interpret an accident report

☐ Identify unsafe working conditions

☐ Talk about safety

☐ Prepare for an interview

Go to MyEnglishLab for more practice after each lesson.

Matt Molino

Matt *Today*
One of my warehouse guys just had an accident! Luckily, he's going to be OK. But I need to look into this.

89

LISTENING AND SPEAKING

1 Describe an accident

GET READY TO WATCH

Matt is reporting a workplace accident to Gary. Have you ever witnessed a workplace accident?

WATCH

■◀ **Watch the video. Answer the questions.**

1. Where did the accident happen?

2. What was Steve Warren's injury?

3. When did the accident happen?

4. What does Matt need to fill out?

5. What does Gary want Matt to do now?

CONVERSATION

A ■◀ **Watch part of the video. Complete the conversation.**

Matt: We had an _____ in the warehouse this morning.

Gary: Oh, no. What happened?

Matt: Steve Warren injured his foot while he was loading a _____.

Gary: That's too bad. Is he OK?

Matt: Well, it could have been worse. We called 911, and an ambulance came and took him to the _____. They X-rayed his foot there. It's broken, so he needs to stay home for a while.

Gary: How exactly did he hurt himself?

Matt: I don't know all the details yet, but he was loading 60-pound bags of coffee. Apparently, he tripped and then fell over backwards.

> **Pronunciation Note**
>
> If a word begins with a vowel sound, we usually link it to the word that comes before it. In conversation, we often drop the /h/ sound in words like *he* and *him*.
>
> ◀)) **Listen and repeat.**
>
> Is he OK?
>
> How exactly did he hurt himself?

B **PAIRS** Practice the conversation.

C Read the conversation again. Underline details about the accident.

D **PAIRS** Think about accidents you have witnessed or been involved in.
Write a few details about the accidents. Then have your own conversations.
Student A: Describe an accident.
Student B: Ask questions about it.

WHAT DO YOU THINK?

GROUPS At the end of the video, Gary asks Matt to meet with Kelly about the accident. Why does he do that? Do you think he is right to be concerned?

2

Reflexive pronouns

STUDY Reflexive Pronouns

Singular: myself, yourself, himself, herself, itself	Plural: ourselves, yourselves, themselves
He hurt **himself** when he fell down this morning.	
I felt sorry for **myself** after I broke my leg.	
They were able to find the restaurant **by themselves**.	

> **Grammar Note**
>
> - Use a reflexive pronoun as the object of a verb or preposition when the subject and the object of a sentence are the same.
> - *By* + a reflexive pronoun means "alone."

PRACTICE

A Complete the paragraph with reflexive pronouns.

We all need to take better care of (1) _____*ourselves*_____ in the workplace.
People injure (2) _____ at work too often. For example, Nadia burned
(3) _____ while she was frying hamburgers in a fast food restaurant.
Manuel cut (4) _____ while he was slicing cardboard in a factory.
Both Nadia and Manuel promised (5) _____ they would be more
careful in the future. But it's also the responsibility of each workplace to look carefully
at (6) _____ and make sure that it is providing safe conditions for
its workers.

B Complete the sentences. Use the words from the box and reflexive pronouns.

> angry at ~~introduced~~ live by proud of taught walk by

1. The nurse _*introduced herself*_ to the patient before she treated his injury.
2. After I slipped on the ice and broke my hip, I was _____ for not being more careful.
3. If you can _____, you probably don't need a wheelchair.
4. Eric _____ how to play the guitar, and he's really good now.
5. When Anh was accepted into the program, she felt _____ for all her hard work.
6. My parents _____ in a small apartment, even though they are in their 90s.

WHAT ABOUT YOU?

GROUPS Ask and answer the questions using reflexive pronouns.

1. Have you ever taught yourself how to do something? What?
2. When have you felt proud of yourself?
3. What do you do by yourself?

I taught myself how to bake cakes.

3 Interpret an accident report

GET READY

Matt is reviewing an accident report. Have you ever read or had to fill out an accident report?

PRACTICAL READING

 A **Read the accident report. Where did the accident happen?**

Accident Report

Date of event: _3/21/2014_   Time of event: _4:35 p.m._

Exact location of event: _It occurred in the warehouse office._

What part of the body was injured? Describe in detail. _The lower back_

What was the nature of the injury? Describe in detail. _The employee sprained a muscle in her lower back._

Describe fully how the accident happened. What was the employee doing prior to the event? What equipment or tools were being used? _The employee was lifting a box of paper in order to carry it over to the office printer. She cried out in pain and dropped the box. She was not using any equipment or tools at the time._

Names of all witnesses: _Greg Arkady_

Were safety regulations in place and followed? _Ms. Baxter is an office employee, so she did not receive the training in how to lift materials safely that we usually give our warehouse employees. She had not taken a break that day prior to the event, so fatigue may have been a factor in the accident._

Did the employee receive medical attention? Give doctor's name and hospital. _Yes, she was in a lot of pain, so we called an ambulance. She was taken to Jackson Memorial Hospital and was treated by Dr. Ramón Mendez. A copy of his report is attached._

Injured person's signature: _Wanda Baxter_

Prepared by: _Matt Molino_   Date: _3/21/2014_

B Read the report again. Complete the sentences with the words from the box.

(fatigue   fully   occur   prior to   regulations   sprain)

1. There were no safety _____ posted about using the equipment.

2. _____ this accident, there had never been an accident at the company.

3. It is important for the supervisor to describe the accident _____.

4. It is unusual for an accident to _____ in the employee break room.

5. Kay is recovering from a back _____, so she can't work for a few weeks.

6. Ben hasn't been sleeping enough, and _____ is causing him to make mistakes.

C Read the accident report again. Answer the questions.

1. Who had an accident?

2. When did the accident happen?

3. Where were the victim's injuries?

4. How did the accident happen?

5. Who saw the accident?

6. How did the injured person get to the hospital?

PRACTICAL LISTENING

◀))) Listen to the radio report on common workplace injuries. Answer the questions.

1. In which three workplaces do most workplace injuries occur?

2. Which occupations have the greatest number of injuries?

3. Why are nursing aides injured a lot?

4. What is the most common type of workplace injury? Which part of the body is most affected?

5. What are three other common causes of workplace injuries?

6. What does the report recommend that employers do to prevent accidents?

WHAT DO YOU THINK?

GROUPS Think about the information in the accident report and the radio report on common workplace accidents. Discuss: Why did Wanda Baxter's accident happen? What could Traven Global Coffee do to prevent this type of accident from happening again?

4

Identify unsafe working conditions

GET READY TO WATCH

Matt is discussing the accident with Kelly from HR. Do you know what steps managers in a workplace are supposed to take after an accident happens?

WATCH

■◀ **Watch the video. Answer the questions.**

1. How many accidents happened in the warehouse in the past? What about now?
2. What do people do when they rush, according to Matt?
3. Why does Matt think the reorganization may have caused the accident?
4. What does Kelly think they need to do now?

CONVERSATION

A ■◀ **Watch part of the video. Complete the conversation.**

Kelly: Why are these accidents happening?

Matt: Well, one thought occurred to me. We've been asking the workers to pick up the pace lately. When people

_____, they're less careful than they should be. . . .

Kelly: . . . and they make mistakes, and have accidents. When did you start asking the staff to work faster?

Matt: A couple of months ago. That's when we started getting all those big new orders.

Kelly: The connection seems pretty clear to me. If we hadn't asked the guys to work faster,

the _____ rate wouldn't have gone up.

Matt: I agree. But I don't think that's the whole story. The warehouse reorganization may also be an issue.

Kelly: Really? I thought the reorganization had made the warehouse more efficient.

Matt: It has, but we're using the space differently. We also bought some new

_____. The guys aren't really used to everything yet.

> **Pronunciation Note**
>
> In many unstressed syllables and short words, we pronounce the vowel as the very short, unclear sound /ə/.
>
> ◀)) **Listen and repeat.**
>
> a couple of months ago
>
> The connection seems clear to me.

B **PAIRS** Practice the conversation.

C Read the conversation again. Underline the places where Matt reports unsafe working conditions.

D **PAIRS** Think about an accident that you experienced or witnessed. Write the unsafe conditions that you think caused it. Then have your own conversations. Talk about unsafe conditions that caused accidents.

WHAT DO YOU THINK?

GROUPS In the video, Matt says that the warehouse reorganization caused the accident. Can you think of situations in which changes at home, school, or in a workplace caused accidents?

5

Past unreal conditional

STUDY Past Unreal Conditional

if Clause	Result Clause
If you **hadn't lifted** that heavy box,	you **wouldn't have injured** your back.
If they **had followed** safety regulations,	they **would have had** fewer accidents.
If we **had known** you were coming,	we **would have bought** more food.

Grammar Note

· Use the *if* clause + past perfect to talk about unreal situations in the past.
  It describes what would have happened if circumstances had been different.
· If the *if* clause follows the result clause, there is no comma:
  You wouldn't have injured your back if you hadn't lifted that heavy box.

PRACTICE

A Complete the sentences. Use the past unreal conditional form of the verbs.

1. If we ___had known___ the machine was dangerous, we _____ using it.
   know   stop

2. I _____ him to use the equipment if I _____ him well.
   not / allow   not / train

3. If the accident _____ worse, we _____ it to Human Resources.
   be   report

4. They _____ Pablo to the ER if he _____ his leg.
   take   break

5. Hong _____ if the landlord _____ the stairs in her building.
   not / trip   fix

6. If it _____ last night, I _____ the car into a tree.
   not / snow   not / crash

B Combine the two sentences using the past unreal conditional. Use a separate piece of paper.

1. I didn't have enough money. I didn't buy the computer.

> *If I had had enough money, I would have bought the computer.*

2. You didn't work overtime. You didn't finish the project.

3. We didn't leave the house early enough. We were late for the concert.

4. He lost his job. He moved to another city.

5. She worked in a restaurant. She decided to become a chef.

WHAT ABOUT YOU?

PAIRS Think about things that happened in the past. Based on what you know now, what would you have done or what would have happened differently? Use the ideas in the box or your own ideas.

> If I had studied . . .   If I had moved . . .   If I hadn't met . . .

If I had studied harder, I would have gotten better grades in school.

6 Make inferences

GET READY

Matt is reading a magazine article about body language. What do you know about body language?

READ

🔊 **Listen and read the article. Take the quiz. How many of your answers were correct?**

What's Your Body Language I.Q.?

Body language consists of nonverbal gestures, expressions, and body positions. It is a type of communication that all of us need to understand, since research has shown that in everyday communication, 93% of the message is conveyed through facial expression and vocal intonation.

Take the following quiz to test your body language knowledge. For each paragraph, circle *True* or *False*.

1. While you are interviewing a job applicant, you inquire about her most recent position. She reacts by avoiding eye contact, hiding her mouth with her hands and breathing more rapidly. She must be lying about something.	True	False
2. Smiling is an appropriate response in almost all situations because it demonstrates that you are friendly, outgoing, and easy to get along with.	True	False
3. When someone crosses both arms in front of his body, it may convey that he is very firm and unmovable in his attitude, but it can also indicate that he is deep in thought about something.	True	False
4. If someone nods her head while listening to you, she is confirming that she understands what you are trying to communicate.	True	False
5. People who touch their hair a lot are revealing that they feel anxious and ill-at-ease.	True	False
6. When a person faces you with his head tilted slightly to the side, it indicates that he is paying close attention to you.	True	False

Answers

1. False. While certain signals can imply that someone is lying, the same signals may also be displayed by a person who is nervous. Don't jump to conclusions. In this situation, you also don't want the interview to get off on the wrong foot, so you should ask more questions to confirm your observations.

2. False. Smiling can make a positive impression, but it's not a good idea to go overboard. In fact, if you smile excessively, it can rub people the wrong way. It may lead them to conclude that you are embarrassed, tense, or trying to be humorous.

3. True. A single gesture can signify a variety of different things. Therefore, when you attempt to interpret nonverbal communication, it's imperative to consider all the different types of body language a person is displaying rather than focusing on one gesture.

4. True. Nodding the head confirms that the listener is in agreement with the speaker, but keep in mind that excessive nodding can indicate that the listener is trying to please the speaker.

5. False. Although hair touching can be a nervous habit, it is also possible that the person is trying to flirt with you.

6. True. Head tilting is generally an indication that the person is hanging on your every word.

AFTER YOU READ

A **PAIRS** **Read the Reading Skill. Read the article again. For each sentence pair, circle the sentence that is a logical inference based on information in the article. Then discuss why the sentence is a logical inference while the other is not.**

1. **a.** People who avoid eye contact and breathe rapidly are not lying—they are nervous.
   b. To figure out if people are lying, you should both look at their body language and ask them questions.

2. **a.** People sometimes smile a lot when they are embarrassed.
   b. In some cultures, you should never smile because people will think you're embarrassed.

B **GROUPS** **Study the photos. Use what you know about body language to make inferences about how the people in the photos are feeling.**

VOCABULARY STUDY Idioms

Build Your Vocabulary

An **idiom** is two or more words that have a special meaning when they are used together. The meaning of the idiom is usually different from the meaning of the separate words it consists of, so you will need to guess the meaning from context or look the idiom up.

Read the Build Your Vocabulary note. In the article, find and underline the idioms below. Match the idioms and meanings.

Idiom	Meaning
_____ **1.** get off on the wrong foot	**a.** annoy you
_____ **2.** jump to conclusions	**b.** do something too much
_____ **3.** go overboard	**c.** listen very attentively to you
_____ **4.** rub you the wrong way	**d.** decide something without knowing all the facts
_____ **5.** hang on your every word	**e.** begin doing something in a way that is likely to fail

WHAT DO YOU THINK?

GROUPS Do you agree with the article's interpretations of the different types of body languages it discusses? Do you have different ideas about what these gestures, expressions, and body positions mean? Discuss.

ON THE WEB

For more information, go online and search "body language at work." Write two more examples of body language and what they mean. Share them with the class.

Write about unexpected consequences

 GET READY

Matt is reading a blog about workplace changes. Have there been any changes at your workplace or school recently?

 STUDY THE MODEL

A **Read the blog. What was the recent change at the writer's workplace?**

HRINFOSOURCE.com

ABOUT   TRENDS   WORKPLACE   WORKFORCE   BLOG   SEARCH

#WORKPLACE
#Workplace Changes

by Peter Wong on April 25, 2014   5 comments

Many workplaces these days are going through big changes. These changes can cause a lot of stress, and they can sometimes have unexpected consequences. For example, I'm a nurse at a big hospital. We switched over to electronic records at the hospital recently, and we had to deal with some surprising consequences—both positive and negative.

Everyone told us that electronic records would make it easier to communicate with other hospitals, so I expected that. But I didn't expect some other good things that have happened because of the switch. For one thing, we use hardly any paper now because everything is on the computer. Another good thing is that electronic records allow us to work much more quickly. We can see all notes about a patient in one place. We don't have to look through thick patient folders to find information anymore. Also, the new system is very helpful with patient medications. To give a medication, I just scan the patient's identification bracelet. Then my computer shows that patient's exact prescriptions. It also unlocks my medication box. In fact, we haven't had any medication errors since we started using electronic records.

The change to electronic records had some negative consequences, too. One unexpected problem was the extra time we nurses needed to learn the system. We had to work overtime to finish our electronic records each day. No one was happy about that. The first month was particularly stressful. The other problem was that it's possible to make new kinds of mistakes with this system. For instance, I had two patient charts open on my computer at the same time, and I wrote a patient's notes on the wrong chart. My supervisor had to approve the correction. It was embarrassing for me.

Overall, though, the new record system is much better than the old one. Making this change was difficult at times, but I'm glad we did it.

B Read the Writing Tip. Read the Model again. Underline all the phrases that introduce examples.

> **Writing Tip**
>
> Writers use **supporting** details such as **examples** to give more information about their main ideas. Here are some useful expressions for introducing examples:
>
> | | | | |
> |---|---|---|---|
> | *For example* | *For instance* | *such as* | *like* |
> | *For one thing* | *Another thing is that . . .* | *The other problem is that . . .* | |

C Look at the bubble diagram the writer used and complete it with information from the Model.

Paragraph 1:

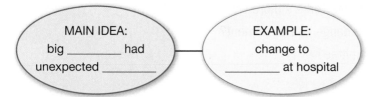

MAIN IDEA:
big _____ had
unexpected _____

EXAMPLE:
change to
_____ at hospital

Paragraph 2:

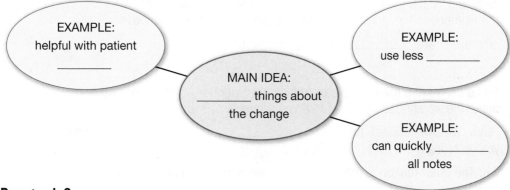

EXAMPLE:
helpful with patient
_____

MAIN IDEA:
_____ things about
the change

EXAMPLE:
use less _____

EXAMPLE:
can quickly _____
all notes

Paragraph 3:

EXAMPLE:
extra _____ needed
to learn system

MAIN IDEA:
_____ things about
the change

EXAMPLE:
can make new
kinds of _____

BEFORE YOU WRITE

A PAIRS Think about a change at home, school, or work that led to consequences that you didn't expect. Make a list of positive and negative unexpected consequences of the change.

B You are going to write about the unexpected consequences of a change. On a separate piece of paper, make a bubble diagram to plan your writing. Use your ideas from Exercise A.

WRITE

Write about unexpected consequences of a change. Review the Model and the Writing Tip. Use the ideas in your bubble diagram. Use a separate piece of paper.

8 Talk about safety

GET READY TO WATCH

Matt and Gary are talking about ways to make the warehouse safer. What is done in your school or workplace to try to make it safer?

WATCH

■◀ **Watch the video. Answer the questions.**

1. What does Matt ask Gary for permission to do?

2. How does Gary respond to Matt's request?

3. Why is Matt going to supervise the workers more closely?

4. What does Matt want to put on dangerous equipment?

5. Who will be on the safety committee?

CONVERSATION

A ■◀ **Watch part of the video. Complete the conversation.**

Matt: Kelly and I think there are a couple of reasons the accident rate in the warehouse has gone up. The first reason is that the warehouse

employees are _____ too fast.

Gary: I see.

Matt: So I'd like to hire more people to reduce staff workload. I think that will make the warehouse much safer. If you approve, of course.

Gary: Hmm. We can definitely bring in some _____. Let me get back to you on hiring more full-time employees.

Matt: OK. The other reason is that some of the workers haven't mastered all the new equipment.

Gary: The equipment you brought in when you reorganized the warehouse?

Matt: Right. So, we think we need to do some _____.

B PAIRS **Practice the conversation.**

C **Read the conversation again. Underline two things Matt wants to do to make the warehouse safer.**

D PAIRS **Make a list of things you want to do to make your home, school, or workplace safer. Explain how these things will improve safety. Then have your own conversations. Talk about improving safety in your home, school, or workplace.**

WHAT DO YOU THINK?

GROUPS In the video, Matt describes plans to make the warehouse safer. Do his plans make sense to you? What additional changes could he make?

JOB-SEEKING SKILLS

Prepare for an interview

Sal Morales   *Today*
I have an interview with Traven Global! Now I need to find out as much as I can about the company.

GET READY

Sal is preparing for his interview at Traven Global Coffee. He is doing some research on the company. Have you ever tried to find out about a company or business?

PREPARE FOR AN INTERVIEW

A Read Sal's company research worksheet. Answer the questions.

COMPANY RESEARCH WORKSHEET

1. What's the name of the company? *Traven Global Coffee*

2. How long has it been in business? Who founded the company?
   Since 1990; founded by Hal and Linda Traven

3. What products and services does the company offer?
   Specialty coffees (roasted on site) and accessories

4. Who are the customers? *Food and beverage managers, restaurant managers, retail managers, direct-buy customers, etc.*

5. How would I describe the company? *Innovative, high-quality products, good environmental practices, dynamic, growing quickly*

6. How many people work there? Who do I know? *About 100 total; Eva Vera, Sales Manager*

7. Who are the main competitors? *Sky Coffee, Shady Mountain Roasters, other small independent roasters*

8. What are the differences between this company and its competitors? *Traven Global is smaller than many of the competitors; their specialty blends are higher in quality*

---

1. Who started Traven Global Coffee, and when?

2. What kinds of customers does Traven Global serve?

3. How many employees does Traven Global have?

4. Which companies compete with Traven Global?

B PAIRS Why is it important for Sal to know about the coffee business and Traven Global's competition?

PUT YOUR IDEAS TO WORK

ON THE WEB

For more information, go online and do a search on the company you chose. Find answers to the questions on your worksheet. Report back to the class.

A See page 159 for a company research worksheet.
Think of a company where you would like to apply for a job. Complete the worksheet with information about the company. Use Sal's worksheet as a model.

B PAIRS Share your worksheet with your partner. What additional questions can you add to your worksheet? Discuss ways to find answers to your questions.

GRAMMAR

See page 151 for your Grammar Review.

VOCABULARY See page 163 for the Unit 7 Vocabulary.

Vocabulary Learning Strategy: Learn Words That Have Different Meanings in Different Contexts

A Choose at least 5 words from the list. Write two meanings for each word on a separate piece of paper. Use a dictionary. For example:

> _strain_   1. a feeling of worry caused by having to work too hard or deal with too many problems
>
>   2. an injury to part of your body

B Circle 5 meanings in Exercise A. Write a sentence for each meaning.

SPELLING See page 163 for the Unit 7 Vocabulary.

CLASS Choose 10 words for a spelling test.

LISTENING PLUS

Watch each video. Write the story of Matt's day on a separate piece of paper.

> There was an accident in the warehouse. Matt goes to Gary's office to tell him about the accident. . . .

NOW I CAN

PAIRS See page 89 for the Unit 7 Goals. Check ☑ the things you can do. Underline the things you want to study more. Then share your information with a partner.

> I can _____. I need more practice with _____.

8 Walt Has an Opportunity

MY GOALS

- ☐ Talk about time management
- ☐ Interpret a meeting agenda and minutes
- ☐ Ask for permission
- ☐ Talk about travel plans
- ☐ Interview

Go to MyEnglishLab for more practice after each lesson.

Walt Soares

Walt *Today*
I have a chance to climb the tallest mountain in North America this summer! I really hope I can make this work.

LISTENING AND SPEAKING

Talk about time management

GET READY TO WATCH

Walt is working at his desk. How would you describe his working style? Does he have problems getting things done on time or not?

WATCH

A ◼◀ Watch the video. Were your guesses correct?

B ◼◀ Watch the video again. Answer the questions.

1. Why did Marie come to Walt's office?

2. What does Walt offer Marie advice about?

3. When is Marie most productive?

4. What does Walt write down every morning?

5. What distractions does Walt mention?

CONVERSATION

A ◼◀ Watch part of the video. Complete the conversation.

Marie: The truth is, I feel a little overwhelmed. Basically, I don't know how to _____ my time here.

Walt: Well, I'm not exactly an expert. But I can give you some tips on how to get things done more efficiently.

Marie: I'd really appreciate that.

Walt: First, save the most difficult tasks for when you're feeling most _____. For me, that's in the morning.

Marie: I'm more of a night owl. Can I come into the office at midnight?

Walt: OK, maybe that tip won't work for you . . . Here's another one. Every morning, plan your day. Jot down a to-do list of the things you need to accomplish.

Marie: Well, I do type notes on my computer screen to remind myself to do things.

Walt: An organized list is better. Then you can _____ the tasks. Always make sure you work on the most important things first.

B PAIRS Practice the conversation.

C Read the conversation again. Underline 2 time management tips.

D PAIRS Think about ways that you try to manage your time and get things done. Write a few time management techniques. Then have your own conversations. Give your partner advice on time management.

WHAT DO YOU THINK?

GROUPS Do you think Walt's time management tips are useful? What are some other time management tips that you could suggest to Marie?

GRAMMAR

Embedded questions with infinitives

 STUDY Embedded Questions with Infinitives

Main Clause	Noun Clause
I don't know	**where to find** the employee handbook.
Laura told us	**how to use** that program.
I can't decide	**when to take** time off.
I didn't know	**whether to go** home or not.

Grammar Note

In embedded questions, the question word may be followed by an infinitive. The meaning of the infinitive is *should* or *can/could*:
I don't know where I can find the employee handbook = I don't know where to find the employee handbook.

  **PRACTICE**

A Complete the sentences. Use the question words and the infinitive form of the verbs.

1. He doesn't know ___*where to buy*___ a new printer.
   <u>where / buy</u>

2. Sam wasn't certain _____ in case of an emergency.
   <u>what / do</u>

3. The intern isn't sure _____ about her schedule.
   <u>who / ask</u>

4. Marisol told us _____ enchiladas.
   <u>how / make</u>

5. I can't decide _____ for the job or not.
   <u>whether / apply</u>

B Rewrite the sentences using infinitives. Use a separate piece of paper.

1. I can't decide where I should eat lunch today.

   > I can't decide where to eat lunch today.

2. Sonny doesn't know who he should hire for the salesclerk position.
3. My boss told us when we could take a break.
4. I wasn't sure what I should do first.
5. Elena asked me how she could fix the photocopier.
6. Li isn't certain where he can buy a new phone.

WHAT ABOUT YOU?

PAIRS Think back to when you were a new student at your school. What didn't you know about the school? Write 4 embedded questions with infinitives. Tell your partner.

I didn't know how to find my classroom.

I didn't know where/when/how/who/whether . . .

Interpret a meeting agenda and minutes

GET READY

Walt is reading the minutes, or written record, of a meeting he attended yesterday. Have you ever read or written minutes for a meeting?

PRACTICAL READING

 Skim the minutes. What was the meeting about?

2014 COMPANY PARTY PLANNING MEETING MINUTES

Location: Conference Room A
Time: April 30, 2014, 4 P.M.
Attendees: Walt, Kelly, Eva, Gary, Olivia, Henry, Ying, and Linda
Minutes Recorded by: Linda

---

1. The meeting started at 4:15 due to the late arrival of a few of the attendees.

2. Kelly gave a recap of last year's company party. The theme was circus fun, and the party was held on Saturday, July 21, from 11 to 4. There were about 75 people in attendance. Kelly's group in HR planned, purchased, and cooked the food, which everyone agreed was delicious. The total cost for food, beverages, and supplies was $850.45, which was within the budgeted amount.

3. Kelly wanted to discuss what could be improved from last year's party. Everyone agreed that last year's July party was too hot, and that it would be better to hold it during a cooler season. Fall weather can be unpredictable due to hurricanes, so Gary suggested that we hold the party in November or December. The tentative date of November 15 was proposed. Everyone will check their department calendars to make sure there are no conflicts.

4. Eva proposed that we give the party a Hawaiian theme. She has a friend who sings in a Hawaiian band, and she will ask if he and his group would like to play for free coffee. Everyone agreed that a Hawaiian theme would be fun.

5. Kelly brought the discussion back to the subject of how to avoid some of the problems from last year. She said that her department enjoyed cooking and serving the food, but they didn't really have time to enjoy the party. Someone suggested hiring a caterer to prepare the food. No one could supply exact figures on how much a caterer would cost. Gary said that in his view, the annual party should be a gift to the employees. It should give everyone an opportunity to relax and enjoy the day together. He suggested increasing the food budget for the party in order to cover the cost of a catering service. Henry commented that it would be fun to have a Hawaiian pig roast, but Kelly objected, saying that quite a few employees do not eat pork.

6. Since it was nearly 5 P.M., Kelly suggested that we table the question of the food and schedule a follow-up meeting at some future date. She will email further details.

7. The meeting was adjourned at 4:55 P.M.

B **Read the minutes more carefully. Complete the sentences with the words from the box.**

adjourned   conflict   recap   table   tentative   theme

1. At the end of a meeting, it is helpful to have a _____ of what has been decided.

2. If a party has a _____, people can more easily plan the decorations for it.

3. We need more information, so let's _____ a decision on this issue until later.

4. I will check my calendar to make sure I don't have a _____ at that time.

5. The _____ date for the seminar is October 2. We will confirm the date next week.

6. Usually the person running a meeting decides when it should be _____.

C **Read the minutes again. Answer the questions.**

1. When did the meeting start?

2. What happened at last year's party?

3. What date was suggested for this year's party?

4. What theme will the party have?

5. What problems did Kelly bring up about the food at last year's party?

6. Why did they decide to have another meeting about the party?

D **PAIRS Read the agenda for the party meeting. Then read the meeting minutes again. Discuss the questions.**

1. Were discussion times assigned for each section of the meeting?

2. Which agenda items were not discussed at the meeting?

3. What decisions were made?

> **Company Party Planning Meeting Agenda**
>
> 1. Recap of last year's summer party
> 2. Propose ideas for this year's company party
> 3. Budget
> 4. Next steps: Assign people to head committees
> 5. Schedule follow-up planning meeting

PRACTICAL LISTENING

◄)) **Listen to a podcast about how to run a focused meeting. Answer the questions.**

1. Why do some people dread attending meetings at work?

2. What information should you put in the agenda for each item?

3. Why should you send the agenda to all attendees before the meeting?

4. What should you do if people are late for the meeting?

5. What should you do if people start talking about other topics during the meeting?

6. What should you do at the end of a meeting?

WHAT DO YOU THINK?

GROUPS Think about the information in the minutes, agenda, and podcast. Do you think the party planning meeting would have gone differently if the attendees had followed the tips in the podcast? Explain your answers.

Ask for permission

GET READY TO WATCH

Walt is asking Gary for permission to do something.
Have you ever had to ask your supervisor for a
special favor? How did you feel?

WATCH

■)) Watch the video. Answer the questions.

1. What does Walt want to do with his brother?

2. What does Walt ask Gary for permission to do?

3. How does Gary respond to Walt's request?

4. What does Walt invite Gary to do at the end of the conversation?

CONVERSATION

A **■)) Watch part of the video.
Complete the conversation.**

Walt: There's something I'd like to ask you.

Gary: Yes?

Walt: I probably should have _____
this up earlier, but I wasn't sure if it was going
to work out or not . . .

Gary: What is it?

Walt: It's really a fantastic opportunity for me. My

brother is organizing an _____
to climb Mount Denali in Alaska. I'd love to join him.

Gary: Oh, I see where this is going . . . you want some time off.

Walt: Yes, if it's at all possible . . .

Gary: How much time?

Walt: A _____.

B PAIRS **Practice the conversation.**

C **Read the conversation again. Underline polite phrases that Walt uses to make his request.**

D PAIRS **Think of things you would like to ask for permission to do at your school or
workplace. Then have your own conversations. Politely ask your partner for permission
to do something.**

> **Pronunciation Note**
>
> In past modals such as *should have*,
> we often link the words together
> and pronounce *have* like the word *of*
> ("should of").
>
> **■)) Listen and repeat.**
>
> I should have (= "should of") brought
> this up earlier.
>
> You could have (= "could of") asked me.

> **Note**
>
> When you ask for permission to
> do something in the workplace,
> phrase your request politely.
> Describe the background to
> your request before making it.

WHAT DO YOU THINK?

GROUPS In the video, Walt asks Gary for a month off. For what reasons do you think
employees should be given lengthy leaves of absence?

GRAMMAR

Past modals

STUDY Past Modals

Subject	Modal	*have*	Past Participle	
I	**should**	have	**told**	you about this sooner.
He	**could**	have	**fixed**	this problem, but he didn't.
You	**must**	have	**been**	happy when you heard the news.
I	**may**	have	**met**	her at a conference last year.

> **Grammar Note**
> · Use *should have* to express regrets about the past.
> · *Could (not) have* can express regrets, possibility, or degrees of certainty.
> · Use *must* or *may* or *might* + *have* to express degrees of certainty about the past.

PRACTICE

A **Complete the sentences with the past modal forms of the verbs.**

1. I ___may have damaged___ the printer when I pulled the paper out.
   may / damage

2. The employees _____ for permission before they left work early.
   should / ask

3. Amy _____ to invite Juan to the party since he's not here.
   must / forgot

4. They _____ us that the storm was coming.
   could / warn

5. Felix got to the airport late, but he _____ the flight because it was delayed.
   might / not / miss

B **Complete the sentences with the past modal forms of the verbs from the box.**

> could / buy   could / not / see   may / not / hear   must / be   ~~should / help~~

1. I missed my deadline. Someone ___should have helped___ me finish my work.
2. I _____ a house three years ago, but I didn't. Now I can't afford it.
3. Ted and Inez aren't here. They _____ that the meeting time was changed.
4. You _____ surprised when you got a new car for your birthday.
5. Ying _____ the accident. She wasn't at work yesterday.

WHAT ABOUT YOU?

GROUPS Read each situation. Then talk about what *should have*, *could have*, *must have*, *might have*, or *may have* happened.

> 1. There was a big storm. Houses and cars were damaged, but no people were injured.
>
> 2. Your jacket is lying on the floor. It has a big hole in it. Your dog is sitting next to it.
>
> 3. In an office building, a window is broken. Several computers are missing.

People should have taken their cars to a safer place.

Differentiate between fact and opinion

GET READY

Walt is reading a blog about fundraising. Have you ever given money to or tried to raise money for a cause?

READ

◀)) **Listen and read the blog. What is the main idea of the blog?**

#ONLINE FUNDRAISERS FOR INDIVIDUALS
#A small way to make a big difference
by Renata Paglia on March 1, 2014 22 comments

If you're like me, someone asks you for a donation several times a week. An international organization is trying to help poor children, or there's been a natural disaster on the other side of the world. I have to confess that I usually ignore these requests because I don't feel a personal connection to or interest in the cause. It may not be logical, but I feel that if I donated, my money would get lost in the crowd of other donations. Also, it might not be used to actually help the people it was intended for. But I've found a truly meaningful way to make donations: small online fundraisers for individuals. With fundraisers like these, people can find out details about a specific person who needs help and then donate money to that person. In my view, it's the best way to make a real difference in one person's life.

Let me give you an example. I've never met Tere Parra, but I know that she is a vivacious and generous 25-year-old from Mérida, Mexico. In June of 2012, her whole life was changed in an instant. While she was visiting relatives in Utah, she fell from a tree and crashed 20 feet to the ground. She suffered many injuries, but the worst was to her spine. She was paralyzed from the waist down. She had to stay in the hospital ICU for three weeks. Then she faced months of rehab . . . and medical bills.

Unfortunately, Tere's parents had no health insurance. Her hospital bills were over $200,000. To help her, Tere's friends and family set up a website to raise money. My cousin from Utah sent me a text about the fundraising site for Tere, and I decided to donate to it. I used my cell to donate . . . it couldn't have been easier. The site raised tens of thousands of dollars, and Tere's friends and family were deeply touched by the generosity of so many strangers. It was awesome to look at photos of Tere, smiling and working hard to regain her former strength, and to know that I had helped.

Small online fundraisers have changed the way I think about making donations. That's why I advise you to look for small causes where your online dollars can really make a difference. Find your own Tere Parra––someone who inspires you to give. I'm confident that you'll discover that making online donations can be a very rewarding experience.

AFTER YOU READ

A Read the Reading Skill. Read the article again. Look at each sentence from the article. Label it *F* (Fact) or *O* (Opinion).

_____ **1.** It may not be logical, but I feel that if I donated, my money would get lost in the crowd of other donations.

_____ **2.** With fundraisers like these, people can find out details about a specific person who needs help and then donate money to that person.

_____ **3.** In my view, it's the best way to make a real difference in one person's life.

_____ **4.** To help her, Tere's friends and family set up a website to raise money.

_____ **5.** I'm confident that you'll discover that making online donations can be a very rewarding experience.

B **PAIRS** Read the Reading Skill and the article again. Focus on the facts. Now discuss your opinion. Do you think donating money to small online fundraisers for individuals is a good thing to do? Would you do it? Give reasons for your answer.

> **Reading Skill**
>
> Writers often mix **facts** (information that can be proven to be true) with their own **opinions** (beliefs or feelings). When you read an article, it is important to differentiate between facts and the writer's opinions. If you focus on the facts, you can form your own opinion.

VOCABULARY STUDY Formal Versus Informal Language

> **Build Your Vocabulary**
>
> In some contexts, such as in official documents, it is appropriate to use **formal language**. In other contexts, such as in online blogs, it is better to use **informal language**. When you learn new words, try to figure out if they are formal or informal in tone so that you will know how to use them appropriately.

Read the Build Your Vocabulary note. Read the formal terms in the chart below. Then complete the chart with informal terms or abbreviations from the blog that have the same meaning. Use words from the box. You will not use all the words.

(ask for   awesome   ~~cell~~   dollars   give   help   rehab   text)

Formal	Informal
cellular phone	cell
benefit	
contribute	
rehabilitation	
solicit	

WHAT DO YOU THINK?

GROUPS Small online fundraisers are one way to raise money for special causes or for people in need. What are some other ways to raise money for these purposes? List some different ways, and discuss the pros and cons of each one.

> **ON THE WEB**
>
> For more information, go online and search "fundraising with social media." Write a couple of examples of successful online fundraisers. Report back to the class.

Write a memo

GET READY

Walt is reading a memo about employee reimbursement for travel expenses. When employees are *reimbursed* for something, a company pays them back money that they spent while working for the company. Have you ever been reimbursed for something at work?

STUDY THE MODEL

A **Read the memo about employee reimbursement. Why is Kelly sending this memo?**

MEMO

To: All Traven Global Employees
From: Kelly Chen, Human Resources
Date: April 30, 2014
Re: Travel Expense Employee Reimbursement

Traven Global Coffee is happy to reimburse employees for business travel expenses. However, it seems that some employees are confused about the rules for travel reimbursement. For this reason, I would like to go over a few of these rules.

Please note the following:

Transportation:
- If your destination is more than 500 miles away, the company will pay for airfare. If it is less than 500 miles away, the company will pay for a rental car.
- The company covers transportation to and from the airport (such as taxi fare).

Meals:
- Traven Global reimburses employees for their own meals only. The company does not pay for meals for customers, family members, or friends.
- We cover breakfast for up to $10, lunch for up to $20, and dinner for up to $25 per day. If you go over these limits on any meal, you must cover the costs.

Hotels:
- Please check with your supervisor before you book an expensive hotel room. Make sure Traven Global will cover the cost of the room before you stay there.
- You must pay for in-room movies and room service at the hotel.

How to get your reimbursement check:
- The first step is to fill out a travel and expense report. Your supervisor must approve and sign the report. Attach receipts for all expenses. Please attach the original receipts if possible. Photocopies are acceptable.
- Submit your report at the end of the month. Unlike in the past, the accounting department will now accept reports only at that time.
- You can expect to receive your check two weeks after you submit a report.

Thank you for your cooperation in following these guidelines. Please let me know if you have questions.

B Read the Writing Tip. Read the Model again. Then underline formal language in the Model.

> ### Writing Tip
>
> When you write, consider the **tone** you want to use. To determine the appropriate tone, think about your audience (the people who will be reading what you write) and the purpose of your writing. If you are writing instructions for a large group of people in a workplace, for example, it's usually best to use a more formal tone.
>
> Here are some examples of more formal language:
> *I would like to . . .*   *Please note the following . . .*   *In order to . . . , you must . . .*
> *Unlike in the past, . . .*   *Thank you for your cooperation.*

C **PAIRS** Read the Writing Tip and the Model again. Why do you think the writer of the Model chose to use a formal tone?

D Look at the outline the writer used and complete it with information from the Model.

   I. Purpose of memo: to go over _____

  II. Transportation:

      • If more than 500 miles, company will cover _____

      • If less than 500 miles, company will cover _____

      • Company covers _____

 III. Meals:

      • Company will cover _____ only

      • Company will cover $_____ for breakfast, $_____ for lunch, $_____ for dinner

 IV. Hotels:

      • Please check with supervisor before you _____

      • You must pay for _____ and _____

  V. How to get your _____:

      • Fill out _____. Attach _____.

      • Submit _____ at the end of the month

      • You will get your check _____ after you submit the _____

 VI. Conclusion: Thank you. Let me know if you have any questions.

BEFORE YOU WRITE

A **PAIRS** Imagine that you are a manager in a workplace or school. Employees, students, and/or others have not been following certain rules that you want them to follow. Write a few important rules or points that you need to explain to these people.

1. Students may use the computer lab from 8 A.M. to 8 P.M.

B You're going to write a memo explaining rules in a workplace or school. On a separate piece of paper, make an outline to plan your writing. Use your ideas from Exercise A.

WRITE

Write your memo. Review the Model and the Writing Tip. Use the ideas in your outline. Use a separate piece of paper.

8 Talk about travel plans

GET READY TO WATCH

Walt is studying a map. Why do you think he is doing that?

WATCH

A ◼◀ **Watch the video. Was your guess correct?**

B ◼◀ **Watch the video again. Answer the questions.**

1. Who is going with Walt on his trip?

2. Why does Walt think it doesn't take much courage to go out in the wilderness?

3. How is Walt going to get to his destination?

4. What does Walt promise to do when he reaches his goal?

CONVERSATION

A ◼◀ **Watch part of the video.
Complete the conversation.**

Eva: So how are you going to get there?

Walt: I was just talking to my brother about that.
The first step is to fly to Anchorage, obviously.
That's the closest commercial airport.

Eva: Are there any direct flights from Miami to Anchorage?

Walt: Nope. We're going to have a _____ in Seattle.

Eva: I see. Then what? How far is Anchorage from Mount Denali?

Walt: It's a two-hour drive to Talkeetna, the nearest town. Most climbers take a shuttle bus to get there from Anchorage. But you can also

take the train, or even a small _____!

Eva: A bush plane . . . that would be so cool! I've always wanted to ride in one of those.

Walt: I know . . . but we're probably going to take the _____.
It's the cheapest alternative.

> **Pronunciation Note**
>
> We often pronounce *going to* as "gonna" when it comes before a verb.
>
> ◀)) **Listen and repeat.**
> How are you going to (= "gonna") get there?
> We're probably going to (= "gonna") take the shuttle bus.

B PAIRS **Practice the conversation.**

C **Read the conversation again. Underline two ways that Walt is going to travel.**

D PAIRS **Imagine that you are going on a trip. Write some details about your travel plans. Then have your own conversations. Talk about a trip you are going to take.**

WHAT DO YOU THINK?

GROUPS In the video, Walt is planning an adventurous trip. What are the pros and cons of taking a trip like that?

Sal Morales *Today*
My interview at Traven Global is today. Wish me luck!

GET READY

Sal is interviewing for a position at Traven Global. What questions do you think the interviewer will ask him?

INTERVIEW

A ◀))) **Listen and read part of Sal's interview. Answer the questions.**

Interviewer: Have you ever made a mistake at work that had serious consequences?

Sal: Sure. I made a pretty big mistake when I first started my bookkeeping position. I was asked to prepare the payroll, so I finished the task as quickly as I could. But after I turned it in, my supervisor found several errors that I should have caught.

Interviewer: And did you learn anything from this mistake?

Sal: Yes. I learned that it's very important to take the time you need with accounting, especially when you're learning new software.

Interviewer: That's very true. . . . OK, on to my next question. Can you describe a difficult situation that you experienced recently at your job and how you dealt with it?

Sal: Well, two months ago our administrative assistant left us suddenly, and we had no one to assist us in preparing the invoices and issuing checks. I had to work quite a bit of overtime until we hired a replacement. But I knew that it was a short-term problem, and I was glad that I could handle it.

Interviewer: All right. Here's my last question: What is a goal that you set for yourself and managed to achieve?

Sal: Well, my goal when I started college was to maintain good grades while working part-time. I think I did manage to achieve that—I graduated with a 3.6 GPA.

Interviewer: I see. How did you do it?

Sal: Basically, I planned what I was going to do in advance almost every hour of every day. I didn't have much free time . . . but I think it was worth it in the end.

Interviewer: Well, I think that's very impressive.

1. What mistake did Sal make at his first job? What did he learn from the mistake?
2. What difficult situation did Sal face at his current job? How did he handle it?
3. What goal did Sal achieve in college? How did he achieve the goal?

B **PAIRS** How well do you think Sal answered the interviewer's questions? Did he show her that he can learn from his mistakes, succeed in difficult situations, and achieve goals that he sets for himself? Give reasons for your answers.

PUT YOUR IDEAS TO WORK

A See page 160 for a list of job interview questions. **Write your own answers to the questions. If you can, include examples and details from workplace situations in your answers.**

B **PAIRS** **Share your questions and answers with your partner. Would your answers impress an interviewer? Discuss ways to improve your answers.**

UNIT 8 REVIEW

GRAMMAR

See page 152 for your Grammar Review.

VOCABULARY See page 163 for the Unit 8 Vocabulary.

Vocabulary Learning Strategy: Use Vocabulary Cards

A Choose 10 words or phrases from the list. Make a vocabulary card for each one.
Write the word or phrase on one side of the card and its definition on the other side.

WORD:	DEFINITION:
accomplish	succeed in doing something

B Choose 5 words or phrases from Exercise A. Write a sentence with each.

SPELLING See page 163 for the Unit 8 Vocabulary.

CLASS Choose 10 words for a spelling test.

LISTENING PLUS

Watch each video. Write the story of Walt's day on a separate piece of paper.

> Marie comes into Walt's office. She apologizes for making him miss a deadline.
> Then she tells him she is having problems with time management. . . .

NOW I CAN

PAIRS See page 103 for the Unit 8 Goals. Check ☑ the things you can do.
Underline the things you want to study more. Then share your information
with a partner.

> I can _____. I need more practice with _____.

9 Kelly Organizes an Event

MY GOALS

- [ ] Convince someone
- [ ] Interpret a workplace policy
- [ ] Organize teams
- [ ] Justify a decision
- [ ] Interview

Go to MyEnglishLab for more practice after each lesson.

Kelly Chen

Kelly *Today*
The big day has almost arrived! This is going to be the best beach cleanup ever. I just hope everything goes well.

117

1

Convince someone

GET READY TO WATCH

Kelly needs Matt's help with a community service day for Traven employees. Have you ever participated in a community service event? What kind of event?

WATCH

■◀ **Watch the video. Answer the questions.**

1. What does Kelly want Matt to do?

2. What did Matt plan to do tomorrow morning?

3. What does Matt agree to do?

4. What does Kelly suggest that Matt's wife and kids do?

CONVERSATION

A ■◀ **Watch part of the video. Complete the sentences.**

Kelly: Henry said he would help me transport all the cleaning supplies to the beach, but he can't make it after all.

Could *you* _____ the supplies at my place at 8 A.M. tomorrow and then drive them to the beach?

Matt: Um . . . can't you take them there yourself?

Kelly: No, because my car isn't big enough. You have a pickup truck, right?

Matt: Yes. . . . I'd like to help, but I'm supposed to take my son

Adam to a _____ tomorrow morning.

Kelly: Can your wife take him? I'm sorry, but this is really important.

Matt: Well, she wouldn't mind taking him. But Adam really wants *me* to watch him play . . .

Kelly: Come on, Matt. Please? I really need this favor. I've already asked three other people.

Matt: Oh, all right, Kelly. I can help you out. I guess it's for a good _____, and I can take him to the next game.

> **Pronunciation Note**
>
> *Can* is usually unstressed and has the short, unclear vowel sound /ə/. *Can't* always has a long, clear vowel sound.
>
> ◀))) **Listen and repeat.**
> I can (= "c'n") help you out. He can't make it.

B **PAIRS** **Practice the conversation.**

C **Read the conversation again. Underline the places where Kelly tries to convince Matt to help her.**

D **PAIRS** **Imagine that you need a big favor. List reasons that could convince someone to help you and excuses that person might have for not helping you. Then have your own conversations.**
Student A: Convince your partner to help you with a big favor.
Student B: Make excuses, then agree to do the favor.

WHAT DO YOU THINK?

GROUPS In the video, Kelly tries very hard to convince Matt to help her. Do you think she is right to do that? What other options does she have to get the supplies to the beach on time?

GRAMMAR

2

Future in the past

STUDY Future in the Past

was/were + going to + Base Form of Verb
I **was going to study** law, but I changed my mind.
They **were going to help** us, but they decided not to.
would + Base Form of Verb
She said she **would come** to the party.

Grammar Note

- Use the future in the past to express the idea that in the past you thought something would happen in the future.
- You can use be + going to + base form of verb to talk about unfulfilled plans.
- You can use would + base form of verb to express promises.

PRACTICE

A Complete the sentences with the correct form of *be* + *going to* and the verbs.

1. Mia ___was going to take___ me to the beach, but she had to work instead.
   take

2. They _____ the park cleanup event, but they got sick.
   attend

3. We _____ to a movie, but our babysitter didn't show up.
   go

4. I _____ my job last year, but I decided to stay.
   quit

5. He _____ a degree in biology, but he switched to chemistry.
   get

6. Carlos _____ to California, but he flew there instead.
   drive

B Complete the sentences with *would* + the verbs from the box.

(buy   cook   give   pick up   ~~set up~~   teach)

1. Jenna promised she ___would set up___ the presentation for us.
2. Gus said he _____ the volunteers from the event and take them home.
3. Tom told us he _____ us how to surf.
4. My boss promised he _____ me a raise next year.
5. Emilia said she _____ dinner for everyone tonight.
6. You told me you _____ me a new computer for my birthday.

WHAT ABOUT YOU?

GROUPS Tell the group about 2 things you once thought you were going to do, but didn't. Then talk about 2 things someone promised you they would do.

I thought I was going to become a doctor, but I became a nurse instead.

My brother promised me he would help me fix my car.

3

Interpret a workplace policy

GET READY

Kelly is reading about absences and leaves in the Traven Global employee handbook. When can employees take time off in workplaces you know about?

PRACTICAL READING

A Read the section from the employee handbook. What kinds of leaves does it mention?

Traven Global Coffee Employee Handbook   **7**

X. Pregnancy and Parental Leave

Full-time employees may take four weeks of paid time off for pregnancy or parental leave. They can take this time off before or after the birth. They do not have to take all four weeks at the same time. Both natural births and adoptions qualify. Both parents may take time off, and if both work for the company, each parent is entitled to four weeks of paid time off. To be eligible for this leave, the employee must have worked for Traven Global for at least 1,250 hours over the past 12 months.

Under federal and Florida state law, parents are protected during their leaves. The Pregnancy Discrimination Act states that it is illegal for an employer to fire, refuse to hire, or deny a promotion to a pregnant woman.

XI. Family or Medical Leave

Under the federal Family and Medical Leave Act (FMLA), qualified employees can take 12 weeks of unpaid leave for family and medical reasons. To qualify, the employee must have worked for the employer for at least 1,250 hours over the past 12 months.

Employees may take this kind of unpaid leave to care for a newborn baby, to adopt a child, or for prenatal care. They may also take leave if they cannot work because of a serious medical condition.

To request a medical leave, the employee must be absent for three consecutive days. He or she must see a physician no more than seven days after the first missed day of work. An employee may also request unpaid leave if he or she needs to take care of a seriously ill spouse, child, or parent.

Leave under FMLA is unpaid. However, an employee may use sick time or vacation time to receive a paid leave.

During a leave, the employer must continue to pay for the employee's health insurance benefits. After a leave, the company must reinstate the employee to the same or equal job position. However, the company does not have to reinstate an employee if the job was eliminated for business reasons.

B Read the employee handbook again. Complete the sentences with the words from the box.

> consecutive   discrimination   eligible   eliminated   entitled   reinstate

1. Certain state and federal laws prevent _____ against pregnant women.
2. When an employee returns from an unpaid medical leave, the employer must
   _____ the employee to his/her previous job.
3. Monday, Wednesday, and Friday are not _____ days.
4. A person who has been employed full-time for 12 months is _____ for
   medical leave.
5. A person on medical or family leave is _____ to insurance benefits.
6. If your job is _____ due to budget cuts, you can apply for unemployment benefits.

C Read the employee handbook again. Answer the questions.

1. How many weeks of paid time off does Traven Global allow for pregnancy and newborn care?
2. When can paid time off for pregnancy or parenting be taken?
3. What does FMLA stand for? Is it a state or federal law?
4. How long does an employee have to work before becoming eligible for FMLA?
5. Can an employee use vacation time to receive payment during leave time for a family illness?

PRACTICAL LISTENING

◀))) Listen to the report about different types of leave. Read the statements and circle
True or *False*. Correct the false statements.

1. National holidays are sometimes paid holidays for employees.	True	False
2. Vacation time is also called sick leave.	True	False
3. All companies give the same number of vacation days.	True	False
4. Most employees have four personal leave days per year.	True	False
5. If you are injured at work, you will receive unpaid leave.	True	False
6. Companies will not pay for days missed due to jury duty.	True	False

WHAT DO YOU THINK?

GROUPS Think about the information in the employee handbook and the report.
Then read each situation. Discuss the answers to the questions.

> 1. Elena is a full-time employee who has worked for her company for two years. She is having a baby next month. Can she take one week of her pregnancy leave before the baby is born?
> 2. Paulo and his wife are part-time employees. They are adopting a child. Can he take paid parental leave?
> 3. Thanksgiving is a national holiday. Will Arnold, a full-time employee, be paid when he takes this day off?
> 4. Ling is a part-time employee. Her husband died. Can she get paid for time off work?

4 Organize teams

GET READY TO WATCH

Kelly and Eva are organizing teams for the beach cleanup. Have you ever seen or taken part in a beach cleanup? What do you think needs to be organized for it?

WATCH

■)) **Watch the video. Answer the questions.**

1. What time will everyone meet at the beach?

2. What will Nancy's team do?

3. What will Walt's team do?

4. What does Eva need to make sure Walt knows?

5. What will Gary do?

CONVERSATION

Ⓐ ■)) **Watch part of the video. Complete the conversation.**

Eva: So we'd better talk about who's doing what on the beach. What do you want Nancy's team to do?

Kelly: They're in charge of _____.
They're going to pick up plastic bottles, beach toys, and anything else that can be reused.

Eva: And they're supposed to use the blue buckets, right?

Kelly: Right.

Eva: OK. What about Walt's team?

Kelly: They're collecting the _____ trash.

Eva: So they're using the black trash bags. What are they supposed to do with them when they're full? Throw them in a pile somewhere?

Kelly: Actually, I had Linda call the sanitation department. It turns out there are a couple

of _____ in the parking lot that we can use.

> ### Pronunciation Note
>
> When we put two words together to make a compound noun, we usually put more stress on the first word.
>
> ■)) **Listen and repeat.**
>
> **beach** toys   **trash** bags
>
> **park**ing lot

Ⓑ **PAIRS Practice the conversation.**

Ⓒ **Read the conversation. Underline the tasks that Kelly has assigned to the different teams.**

Ⓓ **PAIRS Think of events that you can plan with your partner. Imagine that you have a team of people helping you. Assign different tasks to them. Then have your own conversations. Organize teams for an event.**

WHAT DO YOU THINK?

GROUPS In the video, Kelly and Eva organize teams. What factors do people need to keep in mind when they organize teams and assign tasks to them?

STUDY Causatives: *make, have,* and *get*

Active	Management **makes us wear** protective clothing in this room.
	Gary **had the staff join** him in the conference room.
	I **got Ben to buy** the cleaning supplies.
Passive	They don't **have their house painted** very often.
	Did she **get the car repaired**?

Grammar Note

· Use causatives to express the idea that someone causes someone else to do something. *Make* expresses the idea of force. *Have* expresses requests. *Get* expresses the idea of persuasion.
· Use the forms *make* + object + verb, *have* + object + verb, and *get* + object + *to* + verb.
· In passive causatives, there is no difference in meaning between *have* and *get*.

PRACTICE

A **Circle the correct words.**

1. They (had) / made a caterer make food for the office party.

2. I **had** / **got** someone to help me fix my computer.

3. They didn't **get** / **make** me sign a form before I participated in the cleanup.

4. We **had** / **made** the package delivered to her house.

5. Does Carl get his hair **cut** / **to cut** once a month?

6. The police **make** / **have** drivers pull over if they break the law.

B **Use the correct form of the verbs. Put the words in the correct order to complete the sentences.**

1. I ____got my brother to drive____ me home from the hospital two days ago.
   get / drive / my brother

2. Mrs. Ortega _____ at the doctor's office once a year.
   have / check / her blood pressure

3. Polly _____ plant vegetables in the community garden yesterday.
   her neighbors / get / help

4. The government doesn't _____ going to school until they turn six.
   make / children / start

5. Max _____ last week.
   get / dry-clean / his coat

WHAT ABOUT YOU?

GROUPS Answer the questions. Share your answers with the group.

1. What did your parents make you do when you were young?
2. What did someone get you to do for him/her?
3. What do you have done regularly?

My parents made me make my bed every morning.

○○○○○○

GET READY

Kelly is reading an article about the Everglades in Florida.
What do you know about the Everglades?

READD

🔊 **Listen and read the article. What is the main idea of the article?**

Pythons in the Everglades

Every year thousands of people visit the Everglades National Park. This unusual watery ecosystem is one of the largest wetlands in North America. It is also called the River of Grass. Rare birds, alligators, turtles, crocodiles, deer, and panthers—they all call the Everglades home. Some new residents in the Everglades, however, are causing real trouble: invasive species.

Invasive species are nonnative plants and animals that invade an area. They do not have natural enemies in the area, so they multiply quickly. This destroys the delicate balance of the area's ecosystem. The Burmese python, a giant snake, is one of the most alarming new residents in the Everglades today.

How did an Asian snake get into the Florida Everglades? For years, pet stores have imported these snakes into the U.S. from Asia. Some pythons escaped, or pet owners let them loose in the park. Experts first found Burmese pythons in the Everglades in the 1990s. However, they didn't realize how quickly the python population would grow. Within ten years, pythons were a serious problem.

The pythons thrive on the plentiful food in the Everglades. The snake is voracious, and it will eat almost anything. Researchers have found over 25 different types of Everglades birds in python stomachs. Pythons can eat animals as large as deer and are even known to attack alligators. They also reproduce in great numbers. The largest python ever found in the Everglades was 17.7 feet long (5.4

meters). The snake was carrying 87 eggs. Clearly, pythons love the Everglades.

It is impossible to get rid of all the pythons in the Everglades. So, experts are focused on preventing them from spreading. Wildlife officials do not want the pythons to move into residential areas. In 2008, the Nature Conservancy started a very successful reporting program. It's called Python Patrol. The organization trains people how to identify pythons. Drivers often see pythons sunbathing on the roads and highways. They can report pythons to the Python Patrol hotline. Wildlife officials then capture and remove the pythons.

So if you see a Burmese python sunning itself on a road in the Everglades, call the Python Patrol. You'll be doing your part to defend the native inhabitants of the most important wildlife area in Florida from a very destructive invasive species.

Annual Number of Burmese Pythons Removed in and Around Everglades National Park by Authorized Agents, Park Staff, and Park Partners

Year	Number of Pythons Removed
2000	2
2001	3
2002	14
2003	23
2004	70
2005	94
2006	170
2007	248
2008	343
2009	367
2010	322
2012	169

1,825 Total

Number of Pythons Removed
Source: National Parks Service

AFTER YOU READ

A **Read the Reading Skill. Read the article again. For each sentence, write *S* if the sentence summarizes the paragraph and write *D* if the sentence relates an unimportant detail.**

Para 1: The Everglades is called the River of Grass. _____

Para 2: The Burmese python is an invasive species that is destroying the delicate balance of the ecosystem in the Everglades. _____

Para 3: Some pythons escaped into the park. _____

Para 4: A 17.7-foot python carrying 87 eggs was found in the Everglades. _____

Para 5: Officials are trying to stop the spread of pythons in the Everglades. _____

Reading Skill

When you **summarize** a reading, you write a short statement that gives the main information or most important points in it. Details are not included. One way to summarize an article is to first write a summary sentence for each paragraph. Then combine these sentences and reword them to make a clear summary of the article.

B **Write a brief summary of the article on a separate piece of paper. Use the main idea sentences from Exercise A and add additional sentences.**

C **Look at the chart in the article. Does the number of pythons in the Everglades seem to be rising or falling recently? What might be the reason for that?**

VOCABULARY STUDY Connotation

Build Your Vocabulary

The **connotation** of a word is the idea or feeling that the word makes you think of, in addition to its basic meaning. For example, the words *difficult* and *challenging* have the same basic meaning, but *difficult* has a negative connotation, and *challenging* has a positive one. Understanding the connotation of a word will help you understand its meaning more fully.

Read the Build Your Vocabulary note. Then look at the words in the box. Find them in the article and figure out their meanings. Then complete the chart with the words.

> delicate   get rid of   ~~invade~~   let loose   prevent   voracious

Basic Meaning	Positive/Neutral Connotation	Negative Connotation
enter an area	move in	invade
easily damaged, broken		weak, unstable
needing or wanting to eat	hungry	
stop	limit	
take something away	remove	
let go	free	

WHAT DO YOU THINK?

GROUPS According to the article, officials don't think that they can get rid of pythons in the Everglades. Why do you think it might be impossible to do this? What other strategies could officials use to control the spread of pythons?

ON THE WEB

For more information, go online and search "invasive species." Write examples of other invasive species. Report back to the class.

GET READY

Kelly is reading an email from a Traven Global employee. The employee thinks that the company should take part in an event. Have you ever recommended something to your supervisor or coworkers? What did you recommend?

STUDY THE MODEL

A Read the email. What does the writer want Kelly to do?

To: Kelly Chen
From: Jenny Valdez
Date: May 5, 2014
RE: Walk to Cure Diabetes

Hi, Kelly.

I am writing to let you know about an event called the Walk to Cure Diabetes. You may have already heard of it because it's a popular annual event in Miami and around the country. I believe that our company should take part in the walk this year.

There are several reasons why I feel this would be a great event for us. First, diabetes is an important health issue. It affects our community and many of our employees. In fact, I can easily name five employees with diabetes. That means that helping to cure diabetes is an important way to support our community.

Second, the walk will benefit our employees in a couple of ways. Obviously, it will motivate them to exercise more and become healthier. It will also encourage them to bond with each other. The walk is a team event, so employees will work together and have fun as a group. There will be friendly competition between the various Traven teams. Team members will help each other to get in shape for the walk.

Finally, it will be easy to get employees to take part in this walk. The Walk to Cure Diabetes is a very well-organized event. It has a great website, useful tips for teams, and many fundraising suggestions. I believe that the website will make it very easy for employees to sign up. In addition, I walked in the event last year. So, I can talk with employees and encourage people to sign up. I can let them know that the event last year was a lot of fun, even for people who came to watch.

In my opinion, the Walk to Cure Diabetes is a great opportunity for Traven Global. If we join the walk, not only can we help our own employees to work together and stay in shape, but we can also make an important contribution to the Miami community. I hope that you will consider my recommendation. I would be happy to discuss this with you further. In fact, let's take a walk and talk about it!

Sincerely,

Jenny

B Read the Writing Tip. Read the Model again. Underline persuasive language in the email.

Writing Tip

When you express your opinion about an issue in writing, you should use **persuasive language**. This is language that will help to convince the reader to agree with your point of view. In addition, you should give reasons for your opinion, and support each reason with examples or facts.

Here are some examples of persuasive language:

I am writing to . . .   *I believe that . . .*   *I feel that . . .*   *In my opinion, . . .*
We can . . .   *We will . . .*   *Not only can we . . . , but we can also . . .*
Of course, . . .   *Obviously . . .*

C Look at the persuasion map the writer used and complete it with information from the Model.

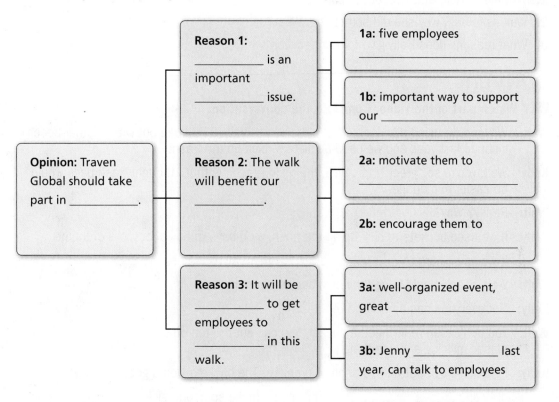

Reason 1: _____ is an important _____ issue.

1a: five employees _____

1b: important way to support our _____

Opinion: Traven Global should take part in _____.

Reason 2: The walk will benefit our _____.

2a: motivate them to _____

2b: encourage them to _____

Reason 3: It will be _____ to get employees to _____ in this walk.

3a: well-organized event, great _____

3b: Jenny _____ last year, can talk to employees

BEFORE YOU WRITE

A **PAIRS** Imagine that you want people at your workplace or school to take part in an event or activity. Think of reasons that could persuade people that it would be a good idea to take part in this event or activity.

Our class should go to a movie together because it's a good way to practice English and . . .

B You're going to write an email to someone in your workplace or school. Express your opinion about an event or activity and try to persuade the person to take part in it. On a separate piece of paper, make a persuasion map to plan your writing. Use your ideas from Exercise A.

WRITE

Write your email. Review the Model and the Writing Tip. Use the ideas in your persuasion map. Use a separate piece of paper.

8

Justify a decision

GET READY TO WATCH

Walt is not happy about a decision Kelly made concerning the beach cleanup. Do your coworkers or classmates ever question you about decisions you make?

WATCH

◼◀ **Watch the video. Answer the questions.**

1. Why aren't Kelly and Walt at the party?

2. Walt asks Kelly why she did something. What?

3. What reasons does Kelly give for her decision?

CONVERSATION

Ⓐ ◼◀ **Watch part of the video. Complete the conversation.**

Walt: Why are we using disposable _____? I helped out with another beach cleanup last year, and we used buckets to pick up the trash.

Kelly: Walt, you're so "green"! . . . Well, the main reason is that I thought trash bags would be easier to manage.

Walt: Really? Why?

Kelly: If we used buckets to pick up all the trash, we'd have to buy a lot more of them.

It would be hard to _____ them all to the beach.

Walt: Well, people could bring their own buckets from home.

Kelly: Not everyone has a bucket at home.

Walt: You don't even really need a bucket. You can cut the top off a plastic milk jug and use that.

Kelly: I guess so . . . but there's another problem. The buckets would get really

dirty and _____. They might make someone sick.

Ⓑ PAIRS **Practice the conversation.**

Ⓒ **Read the conversation again. Underline reasons that Kelly uses to justify her decision.**

Ⓓ PAIRS **Think of a decision that you recently made at home, school, or work. Make a list of reasons someone might think your decision was wrong, as well as reasons justifying your decision. Then have your own conversations.**

Student A: Ask your partner why he/she made a decision.
Student B: Justify your decision.

WHAT DO YOU THINK?

GROUPS In the video, Kelly justifies her decision to use disposable trash bags in the beach cleanup. Do you find her reasons convincing? What would you do if you were the organizer of the event?

Sal Morales *Today*
Does anyone have any suggestions about questions I should ask during my interview?

 GET READY

It is Sal's turn to ask questions during his interview for a position at Traven Global Coffee. What questions do you think he will ask the interviewer?

 INTERVIEW

A 🔊 **Listen and read more of Sal's interview. Answer the questions.**

Interviewer: So, Sal, do you have any additional questions for me?

Sal: Yes, I do, thank you. First of all, I was wondering if you offer your employees opportunities to take training courses, for example, in leadership skills.

Interviewer: There are certainly different courses that you could take online and get credit for. I think the HR department can give you more information about that.

Sal: I understand. . . . And do you pay for overtime hours?

Interviewer: Well, no, we don't pay overtime for this position. You're expected to be able to complete the job during your regular hours. . . . Why do you ask? Do you anticipate that you'll have to work overtime?

Sal: No, no. I was just wondering. . . . Um. . . . of course, this isn't the appropriate time to bring up questions about salary and benefits, is it?

Interviewer: No, we don't discuss those issues at the interview stage. We'll cover all of that if we decide to offer you a position here. But I can assure you that our salaries and benefits are very competitive.

Sal: Yes, of course. . . . So, what's the next step in the hiring process?

Interviewer: We're still interviewing candidates this week. I think that we'll be able to make a decision early next week. So, we'll get in touch with you later in the week if we'd like to make you an offer.

Sal: OK, great. Of course, if you have any other questions, just contact me. And thank you again for the opportunity to interview here.

1. What kinds of training does the company offer?
2. What question does Sal ask about overtime?
3. How does the interviewer answer Sal's overtime question?
4. When will Sal learn about salary and benefits?
5. What is the next step in the hiring process?

B **PAIRS** Read the interview again. Does Sal ask any questions that are inappropriate for a first interview? If so, why are they inappropriate?

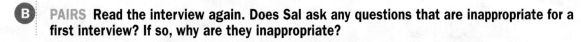

PUT YOUR IDEAS TO WORK

A **Think of a job you would like to apply for. Make a list of 3 questions you would ask an interviewer in a first interview.**

B **PAIRS** Share your questions with your partner. Discuss whether your questions would be appropriate or inappropriate to ask in a first interview. What other questions could you ask?

GRAMMAR

See page 153 for your Grammar Review.

VOCABULARY See page 163 for the Unit 9 Vocabulary.

Vocabulary Learning Strategy: Use Prefixes

A Find words from the list that begin with the prefixes. Fill in the blanks.

dis- (= not):   _discrimination,_ _____

multi- (= many):   _____

mini- (= small):   _____

pre- (= before):   _____

re- (= again):   _____

B Circle 5 vocabulary words in Exercise A. Write a sentence with each word.

SPELLING See page 163 for the Unit 9 Vocabulary.

CLASS Choose 10 words for a spelling test.

LISTENING PLUS

Watch each video. Write the story of Kelly's day on a separate piece of paper.

> Kelly is organizing a beach cleanup event. She stops by Matt's office.
> She tries to convince him to transport the cleanup supplies to the beach. . . .

NOW I CAN

PAIRS See page 117 for the Unit 9 Goals. Check ☑ the things you can do. Underline the things you want to study more. Then share your information with a partner.

I can _____. I need more practice with _____.

10 Gary Reviews the Situation

MY GOALS

☐ Give constructive criticism

☐ Interpret a performance review

☐ Talk about job advancement

☐ Talk about success

☐ Write a thank-you message

Go to MyEnglishLab for more practice after each lesson.

Gary Frye

Gary   Today

Phew! I'm almost done. I'm looking forward to finishing up the last of the performance reviews today.

1 Give constructive criticism

 GET READY TO WATCH

Gary is giving Matt his annual performance review. Have you ever had a performance review at work?

 WATCH

 Watch the video. Answer the questions.

1. What good things does Gary say about Matt's handling of the reorganization?

2. How does Gary criticize the way Matt handled the reorganization?

3. What does Matt promise to do differently in the future?

4. What was even more difficult for Matt than the warehouse reorganization?

CONVERSATION

A **Watch part of the video. Complete the conversation.**

Note

When you give constructive criticism, you tell someone in a positive way that he/she did something wrong. Before you criticize, compliment the person on something. Then provide clear criticism. After the person understands the criticism, compliment the person again.

Gary: I think in general, the reorganization went very well. It was completed on schedule, and it's really increased

the _____ of the warehouse.

Matt: Thanks.

Gary: There were a couple of things that could have been handled a little better, though. For example, I wish you'd noticed that the workers were having problems *before* the accident rate went up.

Matt: Yes, I kind of dropped the ball on that. I was just too busy to _____ the staff closely. There were so many orders we had to fill.

Gary: It *was* really hectic in the warehouse at that time. Nevertheless, for a brief period, the warehouse was not as safe as it should be.

Matt: I know. That's not acceptable, and I've been doing my best to make sure it doesn't happen again.

Gary: I know you have, and I think you've been very  _____.

B **PAIRS** **Practice the conversation.**

C **Read the conversation again. Underline two compliments that Gary gives Matt. Circle Gary's criticisms of Matt.**

D **PAIRS** **Imagine that you are a supervisor, and your partner is your employee. You are going to give your partner constructive criticism on his/her job performance. List two positive comments and one criticism you want to make. Then have your own conversations.**
Student A: Give your partner constructive criticism on his/her job performance.
Student B: Respond to the criticism.

WHAT DO YOU THINK?

GROUPS In the video, Gary gives Matt constructive criticism. Why is it important to compliment people before you criticize them? How could negative criticism affect an employee?

GRAMMAR

too/enough + infinitive

STUDY *too/enough* + Infinitive

too + Adjective + Infinitive
I was **too tired to finish** the job.
The memo was **too confusing to understand**.

Adjective + *enough* + Infinitive
The instructions were **clear enough to follow**.
He is **old enough to drive**. He is **not old enough to vote**.

Grammar Note

· *Too* implies a negative result:
  *I was too tired to finish the job. =
  I didn't finish the job because
  I was too tired.*
· *Enough* implies a positive result:
  *He is old enough to drive. = He can
  drive because he's old enough.*

PRACTICE

A Circle the correct words.

1. She is (hardworking enough) / too hardworking to deserve a raise.

2. The presentation was **interesting enough / too interesting** to be effective.

3. The homework was **too difficult / difficult enough** to do, so I didn't finish it.

4. After the repairs, the building is now **safe enough / too safe** to work in again.

5. I asked for help because the box was **too heavy / heavy enough** to lift.

B Complete the conversations with *too* or *enough* and the correct forms of the words.

1. **A:** Did you ask your boss for a promotion?

   B: No. I was ___*too nervous to ask*___ .

   nervous / ask

2. **A:** Did you like the food?

   B: No. It was _____ .

   salty / eat

3. **A:** Is it cold outside?

   B: No. It's _____ a T-shirt.

   warm / wear

4. **A:** Is Laura using the new software?

   B: No. She's _____ it yet.

   not / well-trained / use

5. **A:** Did you get to class on time?

   B: No. I got up _____ the right bus.

   late / catch

WHAT ABOUT YOU?

GROUPS Talk about 3 things that you are too busy or tired to do this week.
Then talk about 3 things you are smart or strong enough to do.

I'm too busy to go to a movie this week. I'm strong enough to run 5 miles.

PRACTICAL SKILLS

Interpret a performance evaluation

GET READY

Galina Ivanova is a sales representative at Traven Global. Gary is reviewing her performance evaluation. What topics do you think will be covered in the evaluation?

PRACTICAL READING

A **Scan part of Galina's performance evaluation. What ratings did she get in the four main categories of the evaluation?**

PERFORMANCE EVALUATION

Employee: | Galina Ivanova   Position: | Sales Representative

Supervisor: | Eva Vera   Reviewing Manager: | Gary Frye

1. Customer service
○ Outstanding   ● Very good   ○ Satisfactory   ○ Unsatisfactory

> Galina is generally very competent at customer service. She has both a professional manner and a very enthusiastic and friendly personality. As a result, she is well liked by customers. One area that needs improvement is following up with customers after sales. Galina needs to schedule follow-up calls and return calls from customers more quickly.

2. Sales reports and records
○ Outstanding   ○ Very good   ○ Satisfactory   ● Unsatisfactory

> Galina needs to do better in this area. Her sales reports and customer records often contain errors. Also, she turns in her monthly sales reports late almost every month. For the next six months, she should work on improving her accuracy and attention to detail. She also needs to make meeting her deadlines a top priority.

3. Sales goals
● Outstanding   ○ Very good   ○ Satisfactory   ○ Unsatisfactory

> Over the last 12 months, Galina has consistently exceeded sales goals. She is one of our top-selling sales reps.

4. Initiative
● Outstanding   ○ Very good   ○ Satisfactory   ○ Unsatisfactory

> Galina has exceeded expectations in this area. She always takes the initiative in developing new sales accounts. She is creative in how she sells new products. Also, she goes out of her way to accept new responsibilities. In August, for example, she volunteered to cover for another sales rep who was on vacation. There is a strong likelihood that she will grow into a leadership role in the future.

B Read the evaluation more carefully. Then complete the sentences with the words from the box.

accuracy   expectations   improvement   likelihood   manner

1. When I work too quickly, the _____ of my typing suffers. I have to go back and make many corrections.

2. Although the supervisor had high _____ for the new employee, she did not perform very well in the first months on the job.

3. If you have a very good performance evaluation after your first year at a position, there is a _____ that you will receive a raise.

4. After a job performance evaluation, you should pay attention to areas that need _____.

5. Paulo has a very friendly _____, and that makes him a popular employee.

C Read the evaluation again. Answer the questions.

1. What are Galina's strengths in customer service?

2. What does Galina need to improve in the way she serves customers?

3. How does Galina's supervisor feel about her sales reports and records?

4. What does Galina need to do over the next six months?

5. In what area is Galina one of the top sales representatives?

6. What new responsibility did Galina take on recently?

7. What role could Galina grow into in the future?

PRACTICAL LISTENING

A ◀)) Listen to a radio program about asking for a promotion. Answer the questions.

1. Why is it important to ask for a promotion?

2. What sort of performance evaluation should you get from your supervisor before you ask for a promotion?

3. Why should you keep track of your achievements?

4. What do you need to know about the position you want to be promoted to? Why?

5. When is the best time to ask for a promotion? Why?

6. What should you do if your supervisor doesn't give you a promotion?

B PAIRS Discuss. Why do you think that asking for a promotion is stressful? How can being prepared make the situation less stressful?

WHAT DO YOU THINK?

GROUPS Think about the information in Galina's performance evaluation and the radio program. Discuss: Should Galina ask her supervisor for a promotion at this time? Why or why not?

4

Talk about job advancement

GET READY TO WATCH

Gary is giving Eva her performance review. How do you think he feels about her job performance?

WATCH

A ▶ Watch the video. Was your guess correct?

B ▶ Watch the video again. Answer the questions.

1. What does Gary say about Eva's role in Walt's online contest?

2. Why can't Eva take part in the next online contest?

3. What is Eva's new position?

4. What will Eva have to do in her new position?

CONVERSATION

A ▶ Watch part of the video. Complete the conversation.

Gary: I'd like you to be our new regional sales manager for the southern states.

Eva: Regional sales manager! You're kidding, a _____! Wow, I'm stunned.

Gary: Well, you deserve it.

Eva: Thank you so much! Can you tell me a little more about the position?

Gary: Sure. You'll continue to do a lot of things you're doing now. You'll manage a team of sales reps and identify sales goals. The main difference will be that you'll

manage more people and cover a larger _____.

Eva: I understand. Will I need to relocate?

Gary: No, you'll still be based here in Miami. But there'll be quite

a lot of _____ involved. It's important that you and your family be aware of that.

Eva: I think that will be fine. The girls are getting older now, and my parents live nearby.

> #### Pronunciation Note
>
> To show strong feeling, the voice goes up very high and then goes down.
>
> ◀)) **Listen and repeat.**
>
> You're **kid**ding!
>
> **Thank** you **so much**!

B **PAIRS** Practice the conversation.

C Read the conversation again. Underline information Gary gives Eva about the promotion.

D **PAIRS** Imagine that you are a supervisor, and your partner is your employee. You are going to give your employee a promotion. List 3 facts about the new position. Then have your own conversations. Give your partner a promotion, along with information about the new position.

WHAT DO YOU THINK?

GROUPS In the video, Gary promotes Eva. How do you think the promotion might change Eva's life? How can promotions affect employees in both positive and negative ways?

5 Subjunctive in noun clauses

STUDY Subjunctive in Noun Clauses

| He recommended that she **be** promoted to regional sales manager. |
| It is important that everyone **read** this memo. |
| He advised that I **not start** working until the semester is over. |

See page 156 for a list of common verbs and expressions followed by the subjunctive.

> ### Grammar Note
> · Use the subjunctive in a noun clause to express importance or urgency.
> · The subjunctive does not have present, past, or future forms. Use the base form of the verb.

PRACTICE

A **Complete the sentences with the subjunctive form of the verbs.**

1. It's essential that you ____sign____ the form after you read it.
   sign

2. Our supervisor requested that we _____ realistic goals for next year.
   set

3. He insisted that we _____ anyone else about the situation.
   not / tell

4. It is important that she _____ present when we announce the promotion.
   be

5. I advise that you _____ with HR about the benefits you're entitled to.
   check

6. She proposed that I _____ the customers to find out what they want.
   contact

B **Use the correct form of the verbs. Put the words in the correct order to complete the sentences.**

1. Yesterday, the supervisor ___recommended that Mary get___ more training.
   Mary / recommend that / get

2. It is _____ harder if you want a promotion.
   essential that / you / work

3. She _____ for the job at dinner last night.
   I / suggest that / apply

4. It is _____ what is causing this problem.
   vital that / figure out / we

5. At the meeting last week, Mr. Han _____ more careful
   ask that / be / we
   when we work with dangerous equipment.

WHAT ABOUT YOU?

GROUPS Answer the questions. Share your answers with the group.

> 1. What is it important that you do every day at home? At school? At work?
> 2. What do doctors recommend that people do or not do?

It's important that I wash the dishes every day at home.

○○○○○○ **GET READY**

Gary is taking a break. He's reading an interview with a food truck owner.
What is a food truck? Have you ever eaten at one?

○○○○○○ **READF**

◀))) **Listen and read the article. What kind of food truck does Andrew Kim own?**

An Interview with Food Truck Owner Andrew Kim

There's a new food truck in town. Wherever Comida Korea parks for the day, you will find long lines of San Diego food truck fans, twisting down the street like a snake. With millions of food trucks to choose from, what makes chef Andrew Kim's food so special? Our guess is that it's his unique gourmet fusion of spicy Korean flavors and traditional Mexican dishes, all made with locally grown organic ingredients. We interviewed Kim about his popular new business.

What made you decide to start a food truck business?

Well, the restaurant business is in my blood . . . I basically grew up in my parents' restaurant, helping out in the kitchen from a very early age. Of course, I swore that I would never own a restaurant myself because owners work much too hard. Seven days a week, 52 weeks a year! I actually have a degree in urban planning, but jobs in that field aren't easy to come by these days . . . so I was unemployed for quite a while after I graduated a couple of years ago. Then one day, I had lunch at a Chinese food truck, and it was an unbelievable culinary experience. That inspired me to do a lot of research, find a business partner, and buy a truck . . . and the rest is history, as they say.

What's the best thing about having a food truck, and what's the most challenging thing?

The best thing has got to be the customers . . . I just love them. It's so rewarding to watch their facial expressions when they take that first bite. Also, the truck allows me to be more creative with my menu than you can be in a restaurant,

where you're more obligated to serve the same thing every day. The most challenging thing? I have to wear so many different hats: purchasing food, planning menus, taking care of the food prep, scheduling locations and special events, locating good parking spaces, posting daily announcements online, serving the customers, doing the accounting . . . and last but not least, cooking!

What's your most popular dish?

This month, it's our sweet and sour fish tacos. The flavors explode in your mouth!

What direction do you see Comida Korea taking in the future?

I'd love to have an all-vegetarian menu. I know people are crazy about meat, but too much meat in your diet just isn't healthy. But I don't want to beat people over the head with my message . . . so for now, I try to entice them to introduce more vegetables into their diets by offering delicious, creative vegetarian dishes. In other words, I let them discover for themselves how fabulous healthy food can taste.

AFTER YOU READ

A **PAIRS** **Read the Reading Skill. Read the article again. Then read the quotes from the interview. Do you agree or disagree with the ideas they express? Why? Discuss your opinions.**

1. "I swore that I would never own a restaurant myself because owners work much too hard."

2. "I know people are crazy about meat, but too much meat in your diet just isn't healthy."

3. "I let them discover for themselves how fabulous healthy food can taste."

B **Read the Reading Skill and the interview again. Then do the tasks. Use a separate piece of paper.**

1. Write 3 statements of your own opinions about the reading. These can be opinions about Andrew Kim, his business, or his food.

2. Write 2 questions that you would like to ask Andrew Kim about his business.

Reading Skill

When you read an article, you can deepen your comprehension by interacting with the text. **Interacting with a text** means that you think about the ideas and opinions presented in it. Then you decide what your own opinions are about those ideas. You can also think of additional questions you have about the topic.

VOCABULARY STUDY Figurative Language

Build Your Vocabulary

Words or expressions can be used in a **figurative** way. The word or expression does not have its usual meaning; instead, it describes something in a different way to give visual impact or increased interest. Examples of figurative language include similes and exaggerations.
· A **simile** says that one thing is like something else: *Tom eats like a horse.*
· An **exaggeration** is a statement that makes something seem bigger, better, worse, and so on, than it really is: *This is the worst food in the world!*

A **Read the Build Your Vocabulary note. Then read the sentences from the article. Underline the figurative language (similes or exaggerations).**

1. Wherever Comida Korea parks for the day, you will find long lines of San Diego food truck fans, twisting down the street like a snake.

2. With millions of food trucks to choose from, what makes chef Andrew Kim's food so special?

3. Well, the restaurant business is in my blood.

4. I have to wear so many different hats.

5. The flavors explode in your mouth!

6. I don't want to beat people over the head with my message.

B **PAIRS** **Find the figurative expressions in Exercise A in the article. Discuss their meanings.**

WHAT DO YOU THINK?

GROUPS For an inexpensive meal, how would you compare buying a meal at a food truck versus buying a meal at a fast food restaurant? Think of cost, convenience, food quality, and the overall experience.

ON THE WEB

For more information, go online and search "food trucks in [name of your town or city]." Write a few examples of food trucks in your area that you would like to try. Share them with your class.

GET READY

Gary is reading a self-evaluation. An administrative assistant wrote it to describe her own job performance. Why do you think employers ask employees to complete a self-evaluation?

STUDY THE MODEL

A **Read Norma Machado's self-evaluation. Overall, did she have a positive year at work?**

Self-Evaluation

Employee: Norma Machado   **Date:** 9/1/2014   **Supervisor:** Ellen Yates

Please evaluate your job performance over the past 12 months. Include answers to these questions:

- *What do you consider to be your most significant accomplishment?*
- *What duties could you have performed better? What affected your performance?*
- *What is the most important goal that you set for the past year and have reached?*
- *What is a goal that you would like to pursue in the next 12 months?*
- *How can your supervisor assist you in improving your job performance and achieving your goals?*

My most significant accomplishment over the past year has been in the area of computer skills. My job requires me to use word processing, accounting, and presentation software. I am now quite skilled at using these programs, unlike a year ago, when I struggled to perform simple tasks. These days, I can quickly solve most problems that come up, and I know how to find answers to the problems I cannot solve. This has greatly improved my efficiency at work. On the other hand, there are still some complex tasks that I have not mastered yet, and I will continue to work on my computer skills next year.

Even though my computer skills have improved, time management continues to be a challenge for me. I feel like I should have done better in this area because managing my time efficiently is very important in my position. However, I have made some progress. At the beginning of the year, I often fell behind in my work due to poor time management. In contrast, for the last few months, I have been making weekly and daily plans. I have also been prioritizing my tasks. This has helped me, and I hope that I will continue to improve in this area.

My personal goal for the past year was to learn more about accounting. While I feel that I have become more knowledgeable about this subject, I know that I still have a lot to learn. I plan to take more accounting classes at a community college next year.

In contrast to my focus last year on computer skills, in the coming year, I would like to focus on personal skills. Although I am an outgoing person, I feel that I need to show more leadership in my department. Up to this point, I have always followed other people's orders at work. From now on, I would like to start to manage more of my own tasks within the department.

My supervisor has helped me to manage my time better by telling me which tasks I need to prioritize. I would appreciate it if she could continue to do that. I would also like to talk to my supervisor about the possibility of managing more of my own tasks.

B **Read the Writing Tip. Read the Model again.**
Underline the contrastive phrases the writer used.

> **Writing Tip**
>
> Writers often focus on the ways in which certain things or ideas are similar to and/or different from one another. When they focus on differences, they **contrast** one or more thing with another thing.
>
> The following phrases signal contrast:
>
> | | | |
> |---|---|---|
> | However, | While . . . | Although . . . |
> | In contrast, | Unlike . . . | On the other hand, | Even though . . . |

C **Look at the chart that the writer used. The chart contrasts her achievements and goals in the past, present, and future. Complete the chart with information from the Model.**

	Last Year	Now	Next Year
Computer skills	Struggled to	Can quickly	Will continue to
Time management	Was a challenge	Have made some	Hope to continue to
Accounting	Knew very little about it	Have become more	Plan to take
Leadership skills	Didn't focus on this	Follow other people's	Would like to

BEFORE YOU WRITE

You're going to write your own self-evaluation for the past year. You can write about your achievements and goals at work or at school. Review the questions at the beginning of the Model. On a separate piece of paper, make a chart to contrast your past, present, and future achievements and goals. Use the writer's chart as a model.

WRITE

Write your self-evaluation. Review the Model and the Writing Tip.
Use the ideas in your chart. Use a separate piece of paper.

8 Talk about success

 GET READY TO WATCH

Gary has been doing performance reviews all day.
How do you think he feels?

WATCH

A 📹 **Watch the video. Was your guess correct?**

B 📹 **Watch the video again. Answer the questions.**

1. What was Traven Global like when the company first started?

2. What does Gary say that he is proud of?

3. What does Walt say that he feels good about?

CONVERSATION

A 📹 **Watch part of the video. Complete the conversation.**

Gary: We've done a lot of hard work, and it's paying off. We're going

to post some impressive _____ this year.

Walt: That's great. But success isn't only about dollars and cents, is it?

Gary: Well, in my position, the dollars and cents are always part of the picture.
I can't forget about them even for a second.

Walt: I know, I know.

Gary: OK, I'm not completely _____ with money.
I'm also very proud of the quality of the products we make.
I think we launched some truly delicious new blends this year.

Walt: Oh, I agree . . . Sweet Canopy, Mountain Mist . . .
Mmm. This Mountain Mist has got to be one of the
best coffees in the world.

Gary: You got that right. . . . So what about you?
How do *you* define success?

Walt: Well, in my opinion, this company is successful

because of the _____ we've built.

> **Pronunciation Note**
>
> After most sounds, we pronounce the
> -ed ending on verbs as /t/ or /d/.
> We pronounce -ed as /əd/ only after
> the sounds /t/ or /d/.
>
> 🔊 **Listen and repeat.**
> /t/: launch**ed**   /d/: sign**ed**
> /əd/: start**ed**

B **PAIRS** **Practice the conversation.**

C **Read the conversation again. Underline 3 ways that
Gary and Walt feel that they have achieved success.**

D **PAIRS** **Think about what success means to you. List 3 things that you feel good
about achieving at home, work, or school. Then have your own conversations.
Talk about your achievements and what success means to you.**

WHAT DO YOU THINK?

GROUPS In the video, both Gary and Walt are proud of Traven Global's success, but they
measure success differently. Do you agree or disagree with the ways they measure success?
Can you think of any other ways that a company like Traven Global could be successful?

JOB-SEEKING SKILLS

Write a thank-you message

Sal Morales   *Today*
I just sent a thank-you message to Traven Global. Now I have to wait by the phone for their call!

Sal Morales   *Today*
Traven Global called. I got the job!

GET READY

Sal is writing a thank-you message after his interview at Traven Global. Have you ever written a thank-you message? What for?

READ A THANK-YOU MESSAGE

A   **Read Sal's thank-you message. Answer the questions.**

To: eyates@tgc.com
From: salmorales@gimail.com
Date: September 5, 2014
RE: Accounting position

Dear Ms. Yates,

Thank you very much for taking the time to interview me yesterday. I enjoyed learning more about Traven Global Coffee and this exciting position.

The job seems to be an excellent match for my skills and interests. I have extensive experience in business accounting, budgets, and payroll. I possess strong communication skills. I am willing to work both independently and as part of a team. I feel that all of these qualities make me a strong candidate for this position.

I feel a strong personal connection to your company and the products you make. I would very much like to work for Traven Global. You have probably already spoken with Eva Vera, my reference. However, please feel free to contact me if you require any further information. I look forward to hearing from you regarding this position. Thank you again for your time and consideration.

Sincerely,

Sal Morales (305-555-3158)

---

1. How long did it take Sal to send a thank-you message after his interview?

2. What does Sal say about his experience and skills?

3. How does Sal feel about Traven Global and the products it makes?

B   **PAIRS Check (✓) the things that Sal did in his thank-you message.**
- ☐ He said positive things about the company.
- ☐ He reminded the interviewer about his qualifications for the position.
- ☐ He asked more questions about the position.
- ☐ He mentioned something that he forgot to tell the interviewer earlier.

PUT YOUR IDEAS TO WORK

A   **Imagine that you have been interviewed for a job. Write a thank-you message to the person who interviewed you. Use Sal's message as a model.**

B   **PAIRS Share your thank-you message with your partner. Discuss how you can improve your message. What changes can you make?**

GRAMMAR

See page 154 for your Grammar Review.

VOCABULARY See page 164 for the Unit 10 Vocabulary.

Vocabulary Learning Strategy: Group by Positive or Negative Meanings

A Complete the chart with words from the list that have positive or negative connotations, or meanings.

Positive	Negative
competent	hectic

B Circle 5 words in Exercise A. Write a sentence with each word.

SPELLING See page 164 for the Unit 10 Vocabulary.

CLASS Choose 10 words for a spelling test.

LISTENING PLUS

Watch each video. Write the story of Gary's day on a separate piece of paper.

Gary is giving Matt his performance evaluation. He tells Matt that in general, the
warehouse reorganization went well. However, he criticizes the way Matt handled. . . .

NOW I CAN

PAIRS See page 131 for the Unit 10 Goals. Check ☑ the things you can do.
Underline the things you want to study more. Then share your information
with a partner.

> I can _____. I need more practice with _____.

PARTICIPIAL ADJECTIVES

Complete the paragraph. Add *-ed* or *-ing* to each participial adjective.

Florida is an excit___ing___ place to visit. There are so many fascinat_____
1.   2.

things to do there. For example, if you are interest_____ in deep-sea fishing, you can
3.

take a boat out on the ocean off of Miami. Some people think fishing is bor_____. Most
4.

of the time, you sit on the boat with your fishing line in the water, and you wait for a fish to

bite. But you'll be thrill_____ if you catch a big fish like a barracuda! Some people are
5.

frighten_____ by barracudas because they have big teeth. If you catch one, try not to
6.

get too close to it! And don't feel disappoint_____ if you don't catch anything. Whatever
7.

happens, you'll have a relax_____ day in one of the most beautiful places on earth.
8.

PRESENT UNREAL CONDITIONAL; *WISH*

Complete the conversation. Use the present unreal conditional or *wish* and the simple past of the verbs.

Matt: What ___would___ you do if you _____ a lot of money?
1. will   2. have

Kelly: If I _____ rich, I _____ buy a big condo in South Beach.
3. be   4. will

It _____ have a great view of the ocean.
5. will

Matt: Oh, yeah? If I _____ a lot of money, I _____ buy a big boat!
6. have   7. will

Kelly: If you _____ a big boat, _____ you go fishing every day?
8. own   9. will

Matt: Well, maybe not every day. But I wish I _____ go fishing more often.
10. can

Kelly: I don't really like fishing. I like cooking. I wish I _____ a better cook, though.
11. be

In fact, if I _____ a lot of money, I _____ hire a chef to teach
12. make   13. will

me how to cook!

MODALS OF OBLIGATION

Complete the memo with modals from the box. More than one answer may be possible.

don't have to   had to   have to   must   must not

MEMO

TO: All employees
FROM: Kelly Chen, HR manager
RE: Health insurance plans

• Last year, all employees _____*had to*_____ select a plan by January 15.
  1.

  This year, if you want to stay with your current plan, you

  _____ select a plan. We will automatically reenroll you in
  2.

  your plan. However, if you want to change plans, you _____
                                                          3.

  select your new plan by January 15. You _____ miss this
                                              4.

  deadline. If you do, we will not be able to enroll you in the plan.

• Sometimes, a life-changing event like the birth of a child happens,

  and you _____ change your health plan on short notice. If
             5.

  this happens to you, you _____ contact Human
                              6.

  Resources as soon as possible.

REPORTED SPEECH WITH MODALS

Read the conversation between Gary and his assistant Luz. Then change the direct speech to reported speech. Use *said* or *told*. Use a separate piece of paper.

Gary said he wouldn't be in the office the last week of March . . .

Gary: I won't be in the office the last week of March because I have to go to a conference in New York on March 22.

Luz: I can book you a flight to New York on Sunday, March 21.

Gary: Thanks. You can also book me a room at the Mayfair Hotel, next door to the conference center.

Luz: I'll try, but that hotel might be full. You should probably stay at the Sheldon Hotel instead.

Gary: I have to be close to the conference center.

Luz: The Sheldon Hotel is one block away, and we can get a company discount there.

Gary: That's fine. You can book me a room at the Sheldon Hotel.

TAG QUESTIONS

Complete the conversations with tag questions.

1. **A:** There's a meeting today at 3:00 P.M., ___isn't there___?

   B: Yes. You won't forget to bring the sales figures to the meeting, _____?

2. **A:** You've finished your report, _____?

   B: No . . . They didn't tell us to turn those in today, _____?

3. **A:** You have to send out these invoices by the end of the day, _____?

   B: Yes, I do. They aren't very easy to process, _____?

4. **A:** Monica can't speak Spanish, _____?

   B: No, she can't. But you can speak Spanish, _____?

5. **A:** You're going to graduate this year, _____?

   B: I hope so. And you'll come to my graduation ceremony, _____?

PAST PERFECT AND PAST PERFECT CONTINUOUS

Read the timelines. Then complete the sentences using the past perfect or past perfect continuous form of the verbs. Use the past perfect continuous form when possible.

Eva's Timeline

1999: — got married, had her first child

2000: — moved to Miami

2004: — received a BA in international business

2006: — got a job as a sales rep at Traven Global

2010: — promoted to sales manager

2013: — enrolled in an MBA program

Linda's Timeline

2001: — received a BA in business

2004: — moved to Miami

2005: — got a job as a sales assistant at Wells Inc.

2008: — got a job as a sales rep at Traven Global

2013: — got married

1. By the time Linda received her BA, Eva ___had been living___ in Miami for one year.
   (live)

2. By the time Linda moved to Miami, Eva _____ her first child.
   (have)

3. By the time Eva started working at Traven Global, Linda _____ as a sales
   (work)

   assistant at Wells Inc. for one year.

4. By the time Eva was promoted, Linda _____ a sales rep for two years.
   _(be)_

5. By 2014, Eva _____ in an MBA program, and Linda
   (enroll)

   _____ married.
   (get)

OBJECT + INFINITIVE AFTER CERTAIN VERBS

Use the words from the box to complete the invitation. Use the correct forms of the verbs.

teach / us / dance	authorize / us / provide	ask / a musician / play
encourage / you / bring	ask / everyone / prepare	~~invite / you / attend~~

Invitation

We would like to __invite you to attend__ our annual company

1.

party on Friday, May 12, from 4:00 to 8:00 P.M. in Conference

Room A. The company is _____ your family to

2.

the party this year. We are _____ a main dish,

3.

side dish, or dessert for a potluck dinner, but the company has

_____ free drinks. We've _____

4.   5.

the guitar at the party, and a dance instructor will

_____ the tango. See you there!

6.

NOUN CLAUSES AS OBJECTS

Complete the conversation between two employees. Tina is a new employee. Change the questions to noun clauses.

Tina: Can you tell me __when I can go to lunch__?

1. When can I go to lunch?

Blake: Anytime between 12:00 and 2:00. You can take 45 minutes.

Tina: OK. Do you know _____ around here?

2. Where can I buy lunch?

Blake: Well, I'm not sure _____ in this area. I always bring my

3. Where are the good restaurants?

lunch to work. But we do have a break room with vending machines.

Tina: Oh, OK. Do you know _____ in the vending machines?

4. What kinds of food do they have?

Blake: Mostly snacks, but there are some sandwiches. Let me show you

_____ on this map of the office.

5. How can you find the break room?

Tina: Thanks. . . . Oh, and do you know _____? I need to talk to her.

6. Who is Terri Vail?

Blake: Sure. She works in HR. It's right this way . . .

MODALS: DEGREES OF CERTAINTY

Employees are chatting in the break room. Complete the conversations with the correct form of the verbs from the box.

> can't / be   could / be   may not / have   might / work   ~~must / want~~

1. **Linda:** The buyer at SuperSave Market left me three messages.

   Eva: Really? He _____ *must want* _____ to make an order!

2. **Nancy:** Where does Peggy's husband work?

   Jim: I'm not sure. He _____ at Jackson Hospital. I know he's a nurse.

3. **Wanda:** Sejun is from Vietnam.

   Frank: He _____ from Vietnam. He told me he was born in South Korea.

4. **Hector:** This vending machine won't give me the chips I paid for.

   Juana: It _____ broken. It was making a funny noise yesterday.

5. **Marie:** I couldn't find any binders in the closet.

   Walt: We _____ any more in there. We'll probably have to order some.

ADVERB CLAUSES: CONCESSION

Complete the paragraph with the clauses from the box and *though*, *although*, or *even though*. More than one answer may be possible.

> he had given them the wrong address   I ordered it two weeks ago
> it wasn't her fault   she had an important meeting   ~~she wasn't feeling well~~

Linda came to work yesterday _*though* OR *although* OR *even though she wasn't feeling well*_ .
 1.

_____ she didn't have any sales presentations, _____
 2. 3.

with a client, and she couldn't miss it. The client was upset. He said, "I'm still

waiting for my coffee shipment _____."
 4.

_____, Linda felt bad about the mistake. She called the
 5.

warehouse and asked them to send the coffee as soon as possible. The company didn't charge

the client for the coffee _____ on the purchase order.
 6.

ADJECTIVE CLAUSES

Complete the conversation with *that*, *which*, *who*, **or** *whom* **and the correct words from the box. If possible, omit the relative pronouns. More than one correct answer may be possible.**

are discussing	contestants can win	I like
live	we've always wanted	~~you suggested~~

Gina: I really liked that contest idea <u>you suggested (OR that you suggested OR which you suggested)</u>
1.
at the meeting.

Luis: Thanks. I hope the managers _____ the idea right now agree
2.
with you!

Gina: I think the prizes _____ sound really cool. Especially the new car!
3.

Luis: The prize _____ the best is the trip to Italy. My wife and I love
4.

Italian food, and Italy is a country _____ to visit.
5.

Gina: Me, too. People _____ in Italy really know how to cook, don't they?
6.

PASSIVE VOICE WITH MODALS

Complete the instructions with the passive voice of the verbs.

16

Photos <u>must be deleted</u> from your digital camera often,
1. must / delete
or you will run out of space to take photos. Before your photos are

deleted, they _____ to your computer. To start
2. should / save
this process, your digital camera _____ to the
3. must / connect
computer. It _____ with a cable, or it
4. can / connect
_____ into the computer's docking station.
5. can / plugged
A folder called "My Pictures" _____ on your
6. should / locate
computer before any photos are copied or deleted. Copy and

paste the photos on your camera into this folder. Your photos

_____ on your computer.
7. will / save
Next, the photos _____ from your camera.
8. have to / delete
Select the photos and move them to the Trash. After that, the

camera _____ from the computer.
9. may / remove

REFLEXIVE PRONOUNS

Complete the paragraph with the correct form of the verbs and reflexive pronouns.

If you're a worker, it's important to _take care of yourself_ on the job.

    1. take care of

Workers can _____ if they don't follow the correct safety

    2. injure

procedures. For example, Zoltan is a construction worker. He didn't wear

his hard hat one day, and he _____ when he hit his head

    3. hurt

on a piece of metal. Linh is a beautician. She _____ with

    4. burn

chemicals while she was dyeing someone's hair because she wasn't wearing

gloves. So you should always _____ at work, especially

    5. protect

if you _____ . There may not be anyone around to help

    6. work by

you if you get hurt!

PAST UNREAL CONDITIONAL

Match each *if* clause with a result clause. Then combine them into one sentence using *I* and the past unreal conditional. Do not use contractions. Use a separate piece of paper.

if Clause	Result Clause
1. be in charge of the safety committee	**a.** not know how to do CPR
2. notice the broken ladder	**b.** provide more safety training
3. not attend the first aid training	**c.** fix it immediately
4. not text while riding my bike	**d.** go to the hospital for treatment
5. not hear Jerry shouting	**e.** not crash my bike into a stop sign
6. break my arm	**f.** not find him lying on the floor

> 1. If I had been in charge of the safety committee, I would have provided
> more safety training.

EMBEDDED QUESTIONS WITH INFINITIVES

Change the sentences with embedded questions to sentences with the same meaning, using infinitives. Use a separate piece of paper.

My boss, "Sam," tried to teach me how to use . . .

Ask WorkBuddy!

Q: My boss, "Sam," tried to teach me how I should use a new software program at work. But for some reason, I can't figure out how I can do the easiest tasks with it. I don't know where I can look up information about the program, and I don't know whom I can ask for help. I can't decide whether I should ask "Sam" to explain everything again. Can you tell me what I should do?
—Embarrassed

A: Don't worry. . . . I can tell you how you should handle this situation. Your boss is on your side. So, you have to learn how you can be honest with him. If you don't tell him what's going on, he won't know how he can help you.
—WorkBuddy

PAST MODALS

Complete the conversation with the past modal forms of the verbs.

Hector: Anya, you're two hours late! You _____ *should have called* _____ me.

1. should / call

Anya: I know. I'm sorry. When I got on the bus, I couldn't find my bus pass.

I _____ it on my kitchen table, but I also

2. might / leave

_____ it in my other purse. . . .

3. may / put

No, actually, I _____ that it was in the pocket of my jeans.

4. must / forget

I was wearing them when I rode the bus yesterday.

Hector: OK . . . but you _____ for the bus with cash, couldn't you?

5. could / pay

Anya: Well, I didn't have any money on me. I _____ money from

6. could / borrow

someone, but I didn't know anyone on the bus. So I decided to walk here.

Hector: You walked all the way? You really _____ me to pick you up!

7. should / ask

FUTURE IN THE PAST

Read the conference planning chart. Then complete the sentences using the information in the chart and future in the past forms.

Volunteer	Task
Sarah	buy snacks and drinks
Ana	prepare the flyers
Oscar and Rachel	set up the booth
Trent, Lee, and Mia	help customers at the booth
Jin and Lucy	clean up

1. Sarah _____*was going to buy*_____ snacks and drinks, but she got sick.
    _{going to}

2. Ana _____ the flyers, but she forgot.
    _{going to}

3. Oscar and Rachel _____ the booth, but they had to finish an urgent
    _{going to}
    project at work.

4. Trent, Lee, and Mia promised they _____ customers at the booth,
    _{would}
    but they arrived late.

5. Jin and Lucy said they _____ after the conference, but they went
    _{would}
    straight home!

CAUSATIVES: *MAKE, HAVE,* AND *GET*

Complete the conversation with the correct forms of the verbs. Add *to* when necessary.

Daria: I moved out of my apartment yesterday. I _____*had my neighbors help*_____ me carry out
_{1. have / my neighbors / help}
all my stuff to the moving van.

Craig: That was nice of them. Did you _____ your apartment with
_{2. get / them / clean up}
you, too?

Daria: Yes, I did! I _____ the floors, and
_{3. get / Ted / mop}
I _____ the windows.
_{4. have / Kay / wash}

Craig: Did your landlord _____ the carpets?
_{5. make / you / clean}

Daria: Yes, he did. But he _____ the microwave that my son broke.
_{6. not / make / me / replace}

TOO/ENOUGH + INFINITIVE

Read part of Bruno's performance evaluation. Then complete the sentences with *too* or *enough*, the adjectives, and the correct forms of the verbs.

Comments:

> Bruno is a hardworking employee, but he needs more experience
> before he can handle a sales position. He knows a fair amount
> about the products we offer, and he can stock the shelves well, but
> he needs to learn more before he can serve customers. In addition,
> he is shy, and he might not be able to talk to the customers
> confidently. Dealing with customer complaints would also be a
> problem for him because he is a little anxious.

1. Bruno is _____ *not experienced enough to handle* _____ a sales position.
   <small>not / experienced / handle</small>

2. He is _____ the shelves.
   <small>knowledgeable / stock</small>

3. He is _____ customers.
   <small>not / knowledgeable / serve</small>

4. He is _____ to customers confidently.
   <small>shy / talk</small>

5. He is _____ with customer complaints.
   <small>anxious / deal</small>

SUBJUNCTIVE IN NOUN CLAUSES

Joe, a supervisor, just gave Dan, an employee, his performance evaluation. Complete the sentences using the subjunctive.

1. Dan sometimes doesn't follow instructions carefully.

   Joe suggested that _____ *he follow* _____ instructions more carefully in the future.

2. Dan sometimes doesn't get permission before he leaves work early.

   Joe asked that _____ permission before he leaves work early.

3. Dan is sometimes not very polite to his coworkers.

   Joe insisted that _____ more polite to his coworkers.

4. Dan and his friend Ed sometimes take three-hour lunches.

   Joe requested that _____ shorter lunches.

5. Dan needs to learn how to use the new software.

   It is important that _____ how to use the new software.

6. Dan needs to come to work on time every day.

   It is essential that _____ to work on time every day.

GRAMMAR REFERENCES

Participial Adjectives Ending in *-ing*	Participial Adjectives Ending in *-ed*
amazing	amazed
amusing	amused
annoying	annoyed
boring	bored
confusing	confused
depressing	depressed
disappointing	disappointed
embarrassing	embarrassed
entertaining	entertained
exciting	excited
exhausting	exhausted
fascinating	fascinated
frightening	frightened
frustrating	frustrated
interesting	interested
relaxing	relaxed
satisfying	satisfied
shocking	shocked
stimulating	stimulated
surprising	surprised
terrifying	terrified
thrilling	thrilled

More rules for reported speech with modals:

Direct Speech	Reported Speech
She said, "**You must** pay the fine."	She said I **had to** pay the fine.
He said, "**We have to** arrive early."	He said **we had to** arrive early.
He told me, "**I will** call you **tomorrow**."	He told me **he would** call me **the next day**.
She told me, "**We won't** let you down."	She told me **they wouldn't** let me down.
He told us, "**I can** pick it up."	He told us **he could** pick it up.
She told me, "**He should** stay **here**."	She told me **he should** stay **there**.

- Pronouns and other words sometimes change in reported speech.
- *That* is optional after both *say* and *tell* in reported speech:
  She said I had to pay a fine.
  *She said **that** I had to pay a fine.*

UNIT 3, LESSON 5, PAGE 39

More rules for past perfect and past perfect continuous:

Past Perfect

Subject	*had*		Past Participle	
They	**had**		**delivered**	the order by the time he called.
We	**had**	just	**finished**	our coffee when you arrived.
I	**had**	already	**graduated**	by 2004.

Past Perfect Continuous

	Subject	*had been*	Present Participle	
By 2012,	Ana	**had been**	**taking**	classes for years.
By the time he quit,	he	**had been**	**working**	at the company for ten years.

- Use time markers such as *before*, *already*, *by (the time)*, *when*, *for*, and *since* with the past perfect and past perfect continuous.
- Do not use the past perfect continuous with *be* and other non-action verbs:
  I ~~had been being~~ worried all day.

UNIT 4, LESSON 2, PAGE 49

More rules for object + infinitive after certain verbs:

Verbs Followed by Object + Infinitive

allow	invite
ask	order
authorize	permit
encourage	require
expect	teach
forbid	tell
force	want
get	warn

UNIT 10, LESSON 5, PAGE 137

More rules for subjunctive in noun clauses:

Verbs Followed by Subjunctive	Expressions Followed by Subjunctive
advise (that)	It is crucial (that)
ask (that)	It is desirable (that)
demand (that)	It is essential (that)
insist (that)	It is imperative (that)
propose (that)	It is important (that)
recommend (that)	It is necessary (that)
request (that)	It is recommended (that)
suggest (that)	It is urgent (that)
urge (that)	It is vital (that)

Complete the job skills assessment list. Give yourself a rating (0 to 3) for each skill.

Rating Key: 0 = do not have skill   2 = have skill
             1 = have skill but need to improve   3 = am very good at skill

Basic Skills	Rating
I like to learn to new things.	
I am good at math. I like to work with numbers.	
I am a good listener. When others talk, I pay attention.	
I am a good writer.	
I am a good public speaker. I enjoy speaking in front of people.	
Critical Thinking	
When I have a problem, I can think about it and find solutions.	
Personal Qualities	
I am confident. I take the initiative.	
I am responsible. I set goals and achieve them.	
Managing Resources and Information	
I manage money well. I don't spend more money than I make.	
I am organized. I keep files in order. I can find information quickly.	
I see the big picture. I can prioritize projects and get things done.	
Social Skills	
I get along with people of different backgrounds and experiences.	
I am a natural leader. I like to guide other people.	
I like helping other people.	
Technology	
I like to use computers and other technology.	
I can fix problems with computers and other technology.	

JOB-SEEKING REFERENCES

Complete the job research chart with facts about three occupations that interest you.

	Occupation 1:	Occupation 2:	Occupation 3:
Location			
Working hours			
Median pay			
Job description			
Skills			
Entry-level education required			
Job outlook, 2010–20			

JOB-SEEKING REFERENCES

Think of a company where you would like to apply for a job. Complete the company research worksheet with information about the company. Add more questions to the worksheet if you can.

COMPANY RESEARCH WORKSHEET

1. What's the name and address of the company?

_____

2. How long has it been in business? Who founded the company?

_____

3. What products and services does the company offer?

_____

4. Who are the customers?

_____

5. How would I describe the company?

_____

_____

6. How many people work there? Who do I know?

_____

7. Who are the main competitors?

_____

8. What are the differences between this company and its competitors?

_____

_____

9. _____

_____

10. _____

_____

JOB-SEEKING REFERENCES

UNIT 8, JOB-SEEKING SKILLS, PAGE 115

Imagine that you are interviewing for a job. Write answers to the interviewer's questions. Include examples and details from workplace situations in your answers. Describe your own experiences if possible.

Interviewer: Have you ever made a mistake at work that had serious consequences? Did you learn anything from this mistake?

You: _____

_____

_____

_____

Interviewer: Can you describe a difficult situation that you experienced recently at your job and how you dealt with it?

You: _____

_____

_____

_____

Interviewer: What is a goal that you set for yourself and managed to achieve?

You: _____

_____

_____

_____

WORD LIST

UNIT 1

Lesson 1
an account
amaze
a barracuda
a blend
land
a shot
stop by
a warehouse

Lesson 3
an attachment
a beverage

a convention
gourmet
host
marketing materials
organic
a price quote

Lesson 4
a bio
culture
immerse (yourself in
    something)
locate

Lesson 6
composition
a feature
the horizon
horizontal
an intersection
a subject
a third
vertical

Lesson 8
appropriate
a brochure

a coffee urn
a discount
an impression
negotiate

Job-Seeking Skills
assess
basic
prioritize
a rating
a resource
take the initiative

UNIT 2

Lesson 1
a concern
a crop
inventory
an issue
make a move
an opportunity
research
stuck with

Lesson 3
clearance event
complimentary
cruise control
fuel emissions
maintenance

mileage
preowned
retail price
VIN

Lesson 4
calculate
a counter
an estimate
pick up the pace
pursue
reorganize
stack
stock up on
supply

Lesson 6
accessible
an advantage
a disability
a disadvantage
interact
socialize
a social networking site
virtual

Lesson 8
benefit
doable
efficient
estimate
in the long run

put together
that settles it

Job-Seeking Skills
analytical
entry-level
a financial record
median pay
an occupation
an outlook
require

UNIT 3

Lesson 1
get the hang of
hands-on
in-house
a rep
software
support
a system

Lesson 3
a cartridge
a description
an invoice
an item number
a purchase order
a quantity
subtotal
tax
total
unit price

Lesson 4
adjust
balance
a commitment
drop out

Lesson 6
a frustration
reflect
reset
a technique

transitional
visualize

Lesson 8
do the trick
on the same page
process
shoot
step-by-step

WORD LIST

UNIT 4

Lesson 1
go live
an intern
keep (something) in
    mind
keep track of
    (something)

Lesson 3
consent
a dwelling
in advance
notice
obtain

renew
a restriction
terminate
vacate
violate

Lesson 4
desperate
maintain
a perk
place (someone)
practical experience
proficient

Lesson 6
an ally
a concept
democratic
develop
establish
a generation
lava
a monument
reflect
wilderness

Lesson 8
administrative
confirm
a form
work around

Job-Seeking Skills
a budget
certify
ensure
in accordance with
a policy
a procedure
a transaction

UNIT 5

Lesson 1
faint
install
a jam
out of order
streaked
toner

Lesson 3
a charity
dedicate to
a donation
fund-raising
a raffle

Lesson 4
approval
balk at (something)
bottom line
impact
an incentive
make up for

Lesson 6
exhilarated
generate
gravity
outdo
plunge

strap in
suspend
a track

Lesson 8
first thing in the morning
give (someone) a hand
have (someone's) hands
    full
phenomenal
stain
take care of (someone)

Job-Seeking Skills
a candidate
consideration
enclose
perusal
a reference

UNIT 6

Lesson 1
all expenses paid
a finalist
a hit
propose

Lesson 3
acquire
a cable
a cord
a digit
display
an extension cord
a PIN

a port
a projector
a wall socket

Lesson 4
a flash drive
give (something) a test
    run
hook (something) up
a slide

Lesson 6
an art gallery
cultural

a delicacy
guarantee
honor
a street festival
traditional
unique

Lesson 8
compromise
a cooperative
document
fair trade
a golden opportunity
the grand prize

publicity
small-scale

Job-Seeking Skills
a contract
documentation
an objective
a reduction

WORD LIST

UNIT 7

Lesson 1
ER
a pallet
a witness

Lesson 3
a collision
fatigue
fully
occur
a physical laborer
prior to

a regulation
a sprain
a strain

Lesson 4
familiarize (yourself with
    something)
occur to (someone)
OSHA
a platform ladder
retractable
stay on top of

Lesson 6
convey
excessive
imperative
imply
inquire
intonation
nonverbal
reveal
tilt
vocal

Lesson 8
caution
demanding
last but not least
promote
a temp

Job-Seeking Skills
accessory
dynamic
found
innovative

UNIT 8

Lesson 1
accomplish
a distraction
jot down
a night owl
overwhelm
save the day
tactful

Lesson 3
adjourn
an agenda
allot
a caterer
a conflict
dread
a recap
table
tentative
a theme

Lesson 4
alternate
bring (something) up
an expedition
a leave of absence
squeeze in

Lesson 6
generosity
paralyzed
regain

spine
vivacious

Lesson 8
a bush plane
indescribable
a mountaineering guide
a novice
a permit
a shuttle
a stopover

UNIT 9

Lesson 1
a good cause
owe (someone) big time
a pickup truck

Lesson 3
adoption
consecutive
discrimination
eligible
eliminate
entitle
federal

prenatal
qualify
reinstate

Lesson 4
a bucket
disposable
a dumpster
a recyclable
refreshments
sanitation

Lesson 6
alarm
an ecosystem
multiply
plentiful
resident
a species
thrive

Lesson 8
company-sponsored
an environmentalist
green
justify
minimize
rinse
unsanitary

WORD LIST

UNIT 10

Lesson 1
capacity
factor (something) in
foresee
hectic
implement
monitor
nevertheless
oversee
a performance review
an undertaking

Lesson 3
accuracy
competent
exceed
an expectation
improvement
initiative
likelihood
manner
a priority
volunteer

Lesson 4
contribute
relocate
a setback
stellar
stun
territory

Lesson 6
be obligated
culinary
entice

fabulous
fusion
an ingredient
inspire
swear
urban planning

Lesson 8
launch
obsessed
post profits

CREDITS

PHOTOS

Cover Photos: Matthew Howe, Photographer. Student Book: All original photography by Matthew Howe, Photographer. Page 12 (left) David W. Martin/Pearson, (middle) David W. Martin/Pearson, (right) David W. Martin/Pearson; p. 13 (1) David W. Martin/Pearson, (2) David W. Martin/Pearson, (middle) David W. Martin/Pearson, (3) Efired/Shutterstock, (4) djgis/Shutterstock; p. 17 Rido/Fotolia; p. 22 (top) deusexlupus/Fotolia, (bottom) zentilia/Shutterstock; p. 26 Karramba Production/Fotolia; p. 31 Rido/Fotolia; p. 40 (top) donskarpo/Shutterstock; p. 45 Rido/Fotolia; p. 55 (left) nicolasdumeige/Fotolia, (middle) Videowokart/Fotolia, (right) NatalieJean/Fotolia; p. 59 Rido/Fotolia; p. 64 (background) tovovan/Fotolia, (middle) haveseen/Fotolia; p. 65 Miredi/Fotolia; p. 68 Xavier Pironet/Shutterstock; p. 73 Rido/Fotolia; p. 82 Gregory Wrona/Alamy; p. 87 Rido/Fotolia; p. 93 auremar/Fotolia; p. 96 (left) Ariwasabi/Fotolia, (right) picture5479/Fotolia; p. 97 (left) WavebreakmediaMicro/Fotolia, (middle) laurent hamels/Fotolia, (right) Monkey Business/Fotolia; p. 101 Rido/Fotolia; p. 110 Stuart Miles/Fotolia; p. 115 Rido/Fotolia; p. 124 Heiko Kiera/Fotolia; p. 129 Rido/Fotolia; p. 138 JJAVA/Fotolia; p. 140 withGod/Fotolia; p. 143 Rido/Fotolia.

ILLUSTRATIONS

All illustrations by ElectraGraphics, Inc. and TSI Graphics.